# IN STILL ROOMS
## CONSTANTINE JONES

the operating system
print//document

IN STILL ROOMS

ISBN: 978-1-946031-86-0
Library of Congress Control Number: 2020933062

copyright © 2020 by Constantine Jones
edited and designed by ELÆ [Lynne DeSilva-Johnson]

is released under a Creative Commons CC-BY-NC-ND (Attribution, Non Commercial, No Derivatives) License: its reproduction is encouraged for those who otherwise could not afford its purchase in the case of academic, personal, and other creative usage from which no profit will accrue.

Complete rules and restrictions are available at:
http://creativecommons.org/licenses/by-nc-nd/3.0/

For additional questions regarding reproduction, quotation, or to request a pdf for review contact operator@theoperatingsystem.org

This text was set in avenir, minion pro, europa, and OCR standard.


Books from The Operating System are distributed to the trade via Ingram, with additional production by Spencer Printing, in Honesdale, PA, in the USA.


the operating system
www.theoperatingsystem.org
operator@theoperatingsystem.org

# IN STILL ROOMS

*for my mother
& her mother
& all the saints*

Αιωνία η μνήμη

— *"Eternal be their memory"*
*Greek Orthodox hymn for the dead*

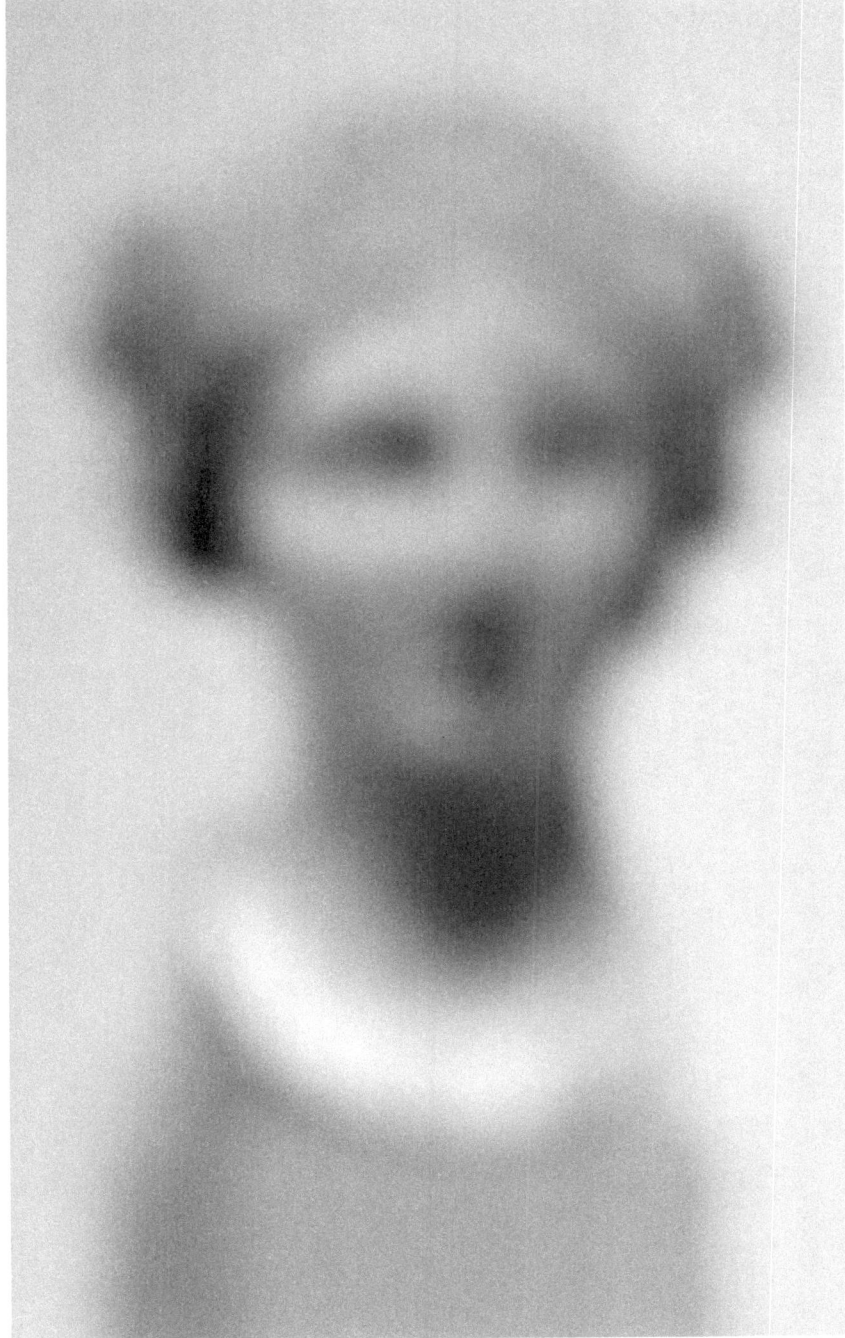

# INSIDE

| | |
|---|---|
| Dramatis Personae | 13 |

## OVERTURE

| | |
|---|---|
| Chorus | 14 |

## ACT I

| | |
|---|---|
| Heirloom | 17 |
| Chorus | 73 |
| Kairos | 75 |

## ACT II

| | |
|---|---|
| Mnemosynon | 83 |
| Chorus | 110 |
| Nostos | 113 |

## CODA

| | |
|---|---|
| Memory Eternal | 121 |

\*

| | |
|---|---|
| Gratitude Pages | 137 |
| Q&A—A Close-Quarters Epic | 143 |
| Bio | 148 |

# DRAMATIS PERSONAE

| | |
|---|---|
| CHORUS | of Southern ghosts in the house |
| ELENI WARREN | 35. Mother of twins Effie & Jr.; younger twin sister of Evan Warren |
| EVAN WARREN | 35. Elder twin brother of Eleni Warren |
| EFFIE | 9. Ephramia Warren; daughter of Eleni, elder twin sister of Jr. |
| JR. | 9. Efstratios Warren; son of Eleni, younger twin brother of Effie |
| SOPHIA KEFALAS | 86. Aunt to Evan & Eleni; younger sister of their mother Evi (now deceased); referred to in the family as *Thea* |
| PARASKEVI WARREN | Evi for short; recently-deceased mother of Evan & Eleni; elder sister of Sophia; grandmother of Effie & Jr.; referred to in the family as *Yiayia* |
| FANOULA SMITH | 45. Fanny for short; Evan & Eleni's cousin, living in a town to the South |
| JOSIAH | 25. Evan's partner |
| KITCHEN | Evan's cat |
| SETTING | An old house at the intersection of Summit & Park in the mountain town of Comona, Tennessee, located on the outskirts of the northeastern-most corner of Tennessee bordering the Blue Ridge Mountains, a region known as the Tri-Cities. |

# CHORUS

We lived in that house before. Died in it too.

Long time ago this was, you wouldn't remember. No, we don't imagine you'd even been born yet. If only you'd of seen it back then—you'd hardly recognize it now, that's for sure. It was a real beauty, that house, back when it was ours. Or suppose we should say back when it let us live there. Maybe you won't understand, or maybe we just can't tell it right. But a house like that, it don't belong to nobody. House like that, it owns itself. And you'd be lucky to spend yerself a couple years under its roof. Least that's how we felt anyway, and you can decide for yerself once we're done.

Thing about that house, like many others in its time, it was a hodgepodge of styles on account of standing so long. Times came and went and families moved in and out and every decade some new little portion was added to the existing body, each generation tacking on their own addition. See the sturdy lumber, how it blooms precisely at the top of this little hill, nothing around for miles save the mountains. In those days it was only three other properties between the house and the Comona Lake to the south. Wasn't til they laid down the railroad did you start to get families coming and settling down. The highway took another good while, and even then we mostly just used the old roads. Least we knew about those. Trusted em to take us where we needed. But through it all somehow, the wars, the riots, the weather, that house still stood. It came up out the ground a fresh white against the sky, and when you looked at it coming up the hill you'd be forgiven for mistaking it one of the Blue Ridge mountains itself, propped up like that against the horizon.

If you'd of asked us back when we was alive do you think this old house'll still be here come a hundred years we'd of never said so. But through all the additions and removals, the comings and goings of we couldn't even tell you how many folks anymore, this house it's still standing. These rooms are still here. And we do suppose we're more'n a little bit proud of that fact. Maybe it don't mean much to you, not yet. But every house it's a strange beast. A house, it's less like a place to live and more like a family itself—all dressed up in its own history, its own secrets. And this house here, it's not done telling itself, not by a mile. Not done remembering neither.

We been part of this house just about as long as we can remember. And we don't resent it none, truth be told. We were there when the walls were white and we were there when they got turned green. We saw the iron staircase sprout from the nursery window upstairs all the way round to the kitchen out back, the little maid scuttling up and down like a bug, rain or shine. Why, that's how old Earlene went, back in her time. Remember that—fell clean off the side of the house, yes she did, broke her poor neck right there on the pavement, isn't that right Earlene. We were there when they stuffed up the attic with insulation, when the walls were stitched through with electricity. We were there when they strung the lights and painted the baseboards, pulled em up, painted em again. When the pipes and the wires came through we made room, and when the wallpaper covered us up we just snuck inside the wood itself. Why, we know that house like we knew our own skin. And it's alive, all right. Only now there's more than one life wrapped up inside. And this one, it ain't like us. We got nobody left to miss us or remember. Not a soul in the world keeping us here. We're only here cause where else would we go, and that's the honest truth.

But now there's another one here with us, stuck between the walls. Hear her moving about at night. We feel her, like a warm vapor. We heard her when she first come, yes we did. Heard her shuffling up the walk and watched her come on back. Cause we always find our way back. Back's the only place we got to go. She came quiet. Like she'd been away a while and was testing the locks. We all felt her come back. Cause when you come back you come back to the here. Don't matter what was there when you was there. Or what's like to be there later on. We're tied to this here. We knew this here back then and we know it across time what it's like to become and still we stay here all the same. Here you are. Here we are, anyhow. And here she was. Not knowing. Not knowing a single thing at all. Knowing only she can't leave. And it's not for us to say whether she wants to or doesn't she. All we know is she's restless. She got to be put at peace somehow. She got to be allowed to rest. All these years and all these folks coming and going and now somehow we got no room at all.

Why don't you just come on in. Have a look around. See it for yourself, why don't you.

# HEIRLOOM

Cold concrete.    A blue like metal  &  all that air
in the air.    The sky clearing its throat
of the smoky Appalachians.
Electric wires cut across the dirt green earth—
those tired metal towers  &  highway grays.    An atmosphere
buzzing the work of the weather    pulling together
a house made of cloud.

.I.

Because she kept checking the window about that loon perched by the mailbox, she let the pot boil over again.

It was supposed to be a nice dinner for Evan tonight; she would fix him something special for the good news. But the loon was making her anxious. Violent birds, those, and scary with their red eyes, that ghostly where are you on the wind. Anyhow, she wondered when the mail would come; she'd been waiting, after all, but surely no one would dare deliver anything with that loon crouched at the streetcorner, its scarlet eye fixed hard on the house. It had come too far from the lake, she thought as she draped a rag over the spill. Even through the kitchen blinds she felt its hot stare, red feathers like war markings across its breast. What business is it got here anyway, she asked the pot. But the pot just kept on bubbling.

She could have kept a better eye on it if Theodora hadn't called—that woman from the church across the state line, in the Virginia half of Bristol. She imagined sometimes the whole Daughters' Association huddled tight around her on the other end of these calls, a flock of old ravens all in their stockings and shawls, shouldering close as they could while Theodora did the squawking. Thirty minutes later, they were still stuck on the phone.

– Ok Eleni, too bad about the luncheon. But we manage just fine. The ladies, you know, we all missing you. How is you Thea Sophia doing.

– Well Theodora you know how it goes. Been hard around here lately, what with all the—. Well, I'm sure you can imagine.

– Be good to see her again, at the meetings. Good for her too sometimes, to be out from the house. You know Mathoula's boy it's a doctor. He says to walk around more, good for the, oh, pos to lei—it helps with the circulations.

Theodora thinks she knows it all, Eleni thought, still stirring the pot. But she's still a village girl like the rest of them, all squabbling in that botched island dialect mixed up with their Appalachian English. No matter what any of their children do, they're still exactly the same—frantic little women from the xorió always talking how bad it is in the states, even though they'd never go back to Greece, not for nothing. They traded their islands for mountains, but they'll never change. Besides they all know about Thea. And still they call like this even when they know. What, they expect we can just hop in some fancy car and drive from Comona around the mountains every Sunday just so Thea can be seen having coffee in the church hall? Got half the mind to tell em not to call anymore, tell em just to cross our number right out the directory. Instead she said simply—

– Well.

– Oh you know what, it's one more thing I forgot. You remember Marina Papadopolou, Dean and Katina's daughter. They friends with you mother and Sophia, back when you father he had the smokehouse. Marina it was like a china doll, the prettiest hair. Maybe you too young to remember. Let me see, how many years—.

– I remember, Eleni lied. What happened.

– So. You never believe. I only heard it from Evgenia the other day, and she only knew because Katina she didn't show to the meeting. And you know how good she is about these things. So Evgenia she calls me, says Theodora, did you hear. I said no koukla what is it. She says it's about Katina, I said my God, what's the matter. She says Marina took a knife from the kitchen, stabbed both her parents right there in the house. Then she ran away. I said Evgenia where did she go, what happened, how could she do that. She said I don't know. They found poor Katina on the ground outside. Dean thank God he was close enough to the phone he could call the nine-one-one. They both in the hospital now, critical condition. Evgenia said she went crazy. I say it's drugs. They all kinds now, everybody, taking drugs. Doing strange things. Evil things. It's the Devil you know. Evil, koukla-mou, all of it. You mother, she knew. Always she was right about these things.

Eleni massaged her temple, knuckled the wooden spoon tighter; she'd stopped stirring the pot. She could see Theodora across the line frantically signing the cross over her breast, all the other Daughters following suit. But it wasn't right, how casually she brings up Mother like that, like she knew her in some special way and wants for me to know. And even if she did, it's only been two years—. Anyway what gives her the right, talking like that. Like the dead are yours to use whenever you got a story to tell. They're just awful, all of them. Every last one of those women.

– That's horrible, Theodora.

– It's the Devil is what it is.

– Mhm.

– You tell you Thea. She knew the Papadopolous good.

– I'll tell her, Theodora.

– You do it.

– I will.

– I call you when I hear something, ok.

– Alright.

– Tell you Thea we missing her here.

Eleni hung the receiver back on the hook, stepped into the light of the window. Outside, the loon was still crouched beside the mailbox on the streetcorner. Look at it looking like that, Eleni thought. What's it want here. Why can't it just go on. Never in my life seen a bird with eyes like that. Not in the Tri-Cities, no sir. Too hot. Too red to be anything but cruel. And those black feathers, those red marks. How come a bird got made to look that way. It's not right. Besides what's it doing all the way out here, so far from the lake. Why's it got to sit there looking like that, just looking at the house, looking and not moving an inch, not blinking, not calling, not nothing. Can it tell the windows are bad, still ruined from the last storm. Can it tell the gutters are loose, drooping off the nails around the verandah. Got to remind Evan to take a look at it. At the little staircase too, from his study out to the backyard. That iron's like to rot clean away one of these days. And with the twins on it all the time I don't trust it. No, I don't trust it one bit. And I don't trust you either. Don't think I don't see you watching this house like it's some tired animal you got a mind to take down. But you'll see. I'll get Evan on the paint again this year. Make it a nice fresh deep coat of green. A green like you never seen before, not this pale olive sick color. You'll see. We'll fix up the place, get that weathervane on the turret above the verandah greased and oiled. And next time you come swooping down it'll follow you with its own metal beak and you'll see. This house isn't some lazy cat come to crouch the end of her days in silence. You'll see this is not a place to feed.

The loon ruffled its oily feathers, lurched into the air, whirled away, carving a slow spiral around the old Victorian.

Down below in the olive house's backyard a small boy shielded his eyes against the glare, wondering what kind of bird that was, flying back towards the lake. His shoe was still caught up in the chainlink out behind the big willow.

This is where he left the treasure, he was sure, in the nook above the second branch. But when he went to check it was only pools of sticky sap. The treasure was gone and now he was stuck. And the dark was coming on quick. He tried not to, but couldn't help looking across the yard at the crawlspace under the deck. For all the crumpled leaves and shadow he knew what slept there underneath the house, behind that little white storage door. His neck hairs pricked up, his skin beginning to goosebump. He felt it watching, and when he turned to look, it was there.

The ick-it.

Just below the deck, in the shade and the dirt, those glowing green eyes. When the light was just right, sometimes he could make out more features, but the ick-it never came out all the way. Sometimes it was an old woman, made of wood, but then she'd turn her head and it was a girl like a marble statue—the face was always changing. Only those green eyes were the same. Familiar too somehow, in a way he didn't like. And the boy knew it was just waiting. He knew that once the sun went all the way down it could come out from under the house with its long hooked fingernails and scrape him under the deck. And he also knew he shouldn't have come out to check on the treasure so close to sundown, but he thought he'd been so clever. His body rattled with fear or anger as much as the cold and he told the willow it wasn't fair but the willow had nothing to say. Suddenly he thought how much better it would be to be a bird.

He was going to try for the laces again but a black shape spilled out from the bushes. At first it put a tight feeling in his chest til he recognized it as Kitchen, the little black cat Evan had found back in Johnson City. He watched her crouch there completely silent on the small deck and wondered, not for the first time, if she knew what kind of danger she was in, that close to the ick-it's cave. He tried to warn her before, but she'd only dart a few feet away, curl back up in some other corner of the deck. Get out of here, he wanted to scream, hoping she would understand. Get out of here, go get Ma, none of us are safe.

– Ma!

He did scream for her, even though she wouldn't hear. But Kitchen heard and knew he was afraid; she twitched her ears and stretched her back and slithered back in through the trapdoor Evan had set into the window for her. That's it, the boy was thinking, I'm done for, I'm caught. But then he saw a different face in the bathroom window upstairs, the circular one they always used to play submarine in. The face was just like his, a little round with brown eyes brown curls big ears all exactly the same only it belonged to Effie not him.

– Effie get Ma! he tried this time, waving his hands at the house.

From inside Effie tiptoed up the stepstool to peep outside the submarine window in case there were giant squids or maybe a mermaid. It was a long time since Jr. went to check on the treasure and she was getting worried. He'll be caught for sure this time, she thought, pressing her nose to the glass. Last time you were up in the tree so long you said don't come follow me so I didn't but still I had to watch til you dropped down. That was back in the summer wasn't it, when the big willow still had her hair. But I can see you now Jr. Your arms make you look like a bug. But this time what if you don't come back at all. What if you're the only brother I have, I won't get a new one. I'll just be with me and I'll never know where you hid the treasure. How does a day without you go, Jr. There's got to be a you cause there's a me. I won't let anything get you, even though you said don't come I have to come, or at least I'll go tell Ma.

Effie clambered down off the stepstool and shot her little legs across the cold tile down to meet her mother in the kitchen.

– Ma! Jr.!

Her mother was stirring the big pot with a wooden spoon and she jumped when Effie slid across the floor in her socks. She'd been staring out the window at the street again.

– Christ Effie you scared the fire outta me.

Sometimes she felt bad about making Ma jumpy and since this was one of those times she looked out the window too cause now she'd made herself a little jumpy. Her mother wrang her hands out on a towel (she told Jr. never to call it a rag one time cause that's an ugly word) before coming over to bend down and brush the hair off her forehead.

– I didn't hear you there baby, stop running through the house, what's wrong.

Effie didn't want to say cause all the sudden she was afraid. Not even afraid of Ma but afraid of the whole big thing. That feeling came back in her throat about being apart from Jr. and she knew if she didn't say anything something bad might could happen. So finally she pointed at the backdoor and just said—

– Jr.'s stuck.

Ma stood back up and the old worry came across her face again. She zipped out the backdoor leaving Effie right where she was in front of the sink.

Effie stared back up out the window. From her height all she could see was the sky, long thin clouds stacked over each other like pulled stuffing. All the orange was just about gone, the window getting that same color blue like in her picturebooks about the ocean, a cold deep color that could swallow anything up. The house was quiet except for a heavy clanging in the foyer, the cuckoo clock's throat going tock tock tock by the stairs. What's that language it's speaking, Effie thought, as she always does when it's quiet enough to hear. The tocking reminded her of a book she used to love, one of the stories Ma would read her after Jr. had worn himself out playing and gone to sleep. In the book there was another little girl just like her, living in a house made of metal in a city of trinkets where it snowed every day of the year. She couldn't remember the whole story anymore but she did remember the clock—a birthday present from the nice old man in the story, a clock in the shape of a pineapple that never needed winding, never lost the time, with a bird inside making the same little songs. What's that girl doing now, Effie thought vaguely as the clouds kept scuffling by. Where did she go, now I'm not there to read about her. She wondered what Ma kept looking for out that window.

The blinds on the backdoor rattled against the glass as Ma stormed in with Jr.'s arm in her fingernails.

– Keep tellin' you not to climb that damn tree! What if you get hurt, what then! I'm in here working hard to get dinner on the table so when Evan comes home we can all eat at a decent hour. Last thing I need is you busting your head open cause you keep hiding your toys in the tree. Efstratios do you hear me!

Jr. looked at the ground but Effie could tell he was trying not to show he wanted to cry. He wouldn't cry in front of Ma, not ever. But she never used their Greek names like that unless they were in trouble, and even still she would always cut Jr. short to Strati, would never use his full name. Effie knew it would be a long walk back upstairs in quiet. Already she was thinking of something to cheer him up.

– Ephramia I'm talking to you too. You shouldn't let your brother run around like that. Y'oughta know better the both of you. Now go upstairs and wait til I call you down for dinner. I don't wanna hear a peep either, you know your Thea's still sleeping.

Their mother watched as the twins hung their heads and walked away in unison. She listened until their footpatter faded across the floorboards upstairs before turning back to tend to the pot. From the corner of her eye she saw Jr.'s boot spilling its muddy laces across the floor where he'd dropped it and for a second she felt bad about having yelled at them. But they just don't understand, she thought as she threw some more salt in the pot, do they Kitchen; the cat blinked once and melted away into some other room. Well, she thought. One day maybe they will.

She looked back towards the mailbox and for a second wondered if it was worth it to go check now that that bird had flown away. Best not to leave the pot all alone again though; she adjusted the flame on the stovetop. Maybe Evan will think to check the box on his way in. Bet that check's been in the mail for weeks already, just the trucks taking their sweet time is all. Just these damn Tennessee roads is what it is. The sauce oughta thickened, she thought vaguely without lifting the cover to see.

She couldn't keep herself from wondering, though, how long did this kind of thing take; it was coming up to the Tri-Cities from her cousin Fanny down in Easton by the river, not a two hours drive away, a favor she hadn't asked for but couldn't refuse. But the mailbox looked a cold lonely thing out on that corner by itself, just sitting there latched shut for no good reason cause nothing ever really came through. Then again, it might could've got lost somewhere, or worse, returned. Fanny might have addressed it to Eleni Warren, simple enough, without thinking this was Thea's house and it wouldn't be the name of their fathers on the address; not the slender Welsh surname they'd both inherited from those wandering brothers, but the Greek name washed over from that little island village neither one of them ever really knew except for Mother and Thea's stories—bleached flicks of dry pathways, hot sandals, donkeys on the rock. What if it had already come and been sent back cause some local postman only saw the name knowing it was Sophia Kefalas, not Eleni Warren, on the house number. A simple enough mistake, cause how's the postman supposed to know anyhow; how's he supposed to see that name and know it belongs to the same family; not to the woman of the house but to her niece; how was anyone at all supposed to know.

She tried not to let these thoughts claw at her. She clenched her fists, that she might crush those small anxieties like eggs. So she tore herself from the mailbox. Instead she looked across the intersection, into the vacant lot, that gutted house across the way, where the storm had left some street sign dipping closer to the turf. Miss Yvonne's house, that used to be. Her mother's best friend. How long ago had she gone, now. And that boy of hers, what was his name. Whole summers running cross the street with Evan as kids just to say hi or deliver some message from her mother and still she couldn't remember that boy's name. Anyhow the place is empty now, he must've up and went somewhere, who can say. A shame, the whole thing. Just look at it now. The winds had knocked a board loose from the window and she could see straight through the glass to the wooden skeleton inside, like somebody'd scooped the house out with a ladle, left the shell of it just sitting there to wait for the weather to take it. No it really wasn't right, that house. Got one foot on the earth and the other in the ground, like someone working a fresh grave and threatening to fall in. How could anyone just let it sit there like that, half a house; weren't there people to come take care of it; she hadn't seen a soul go in or out the whole year. She clenched her fist again.

Further west down the way Park Place extended from her window into a dim gray prick where she could see hooded stragglers dodge their way across the street as if some loose machine might come careening through; as if that kind of thing happened around here. Then came Summit Ave stretching its way south through the intersection toward the lake, the mountains pulling up their purple shoulders in the distance. The road south dipped into a hill, and the houses that way all dropped off into foggy nothing, to where it looked like the mountains had sprout straight up out the air. The way was draped with tired elms and telephone wires, heavy with their news.

Any moment now, she was sure, her brother would come cresting up Summit Ave over that hill. She would hear the bus first—the flush of exhaust in the distance, the electric huff of wheels settling into the stop before it coughed its way away again. Then he would come in his long overcoat up the hill to the corner of Summit and Park; would cross turning east down Park Place towards the house and maybe he would check the mail or maybe he wouldn't but either way I would be able to see him from the window. Any moment now he would come through the door. Any moment he would tell me what was the good news.

Upstairs she heard a heavy thump and silently cursed her children; they knew that their Thea was still asleep. They oughta know better.

Upstairs in their room Jr. slouched in a corner watching the book he just flung away settle in the curtains. Effie stood by their window overlooking the wraparound porch, blinking. There was sometimes a way to get Jr. out of these moods but usually he just had to sit with it. Effie knew it was on account of Ma making him feel small. She felt it too only it always seemed to bother Jr. more. She tried explaining him too—about the submarine window, about his instructions, how she was worried about a giant squid or something else bad happening. She even tried to tell him about the icky feeling of him being gone but she couldn't figure out how to say it good. Don't be dumb, Jr. said and maybe he was right. Maybe it was dumb to be worried or afraid. Maybe it was silly. But she looked at him different now she had him back. If I didn't go get Ma you wouldn't be sitting there, she thought. You'd be not with me. But that's not where I want you. Nine whole years always together and a day without you doesn't make sense. Is there a way to say that, or is it just being dumb. How about the summers when you would unlatch the window to the wraparound and step out onto the roof of the porch, always you first to make sure it was safe. And when I went out myself even if Ma or Evan caught me you would say it was your idea; made them yell at you instead. How do I tell you that's why I went to get Ma, cause you always go out the window first. Maybe that's dumb too. Maybe that's just silly.

Effie picked up the book and sat down across the floor with it in her hands. This one she'd read already, about the little mouse in the castle where everyone ate soup. She offered it to Jr. cause he knew how to say the mouse's name and she thought it would be a way to talk to him, if she asked him to remind her. But he threw the book across the room so it landed in the curtains and now the pages were bent. Still she couldn't remember how to say the mouse's name.

– You think Ma took it.

Effie looked up from the book, confused.

– The treasure, I mean. Do you—do you think Ma took it out the tree.

– I don't think so. Why would she want it.

Jr. shrugged.

– You heard her though. It's like she always knew the secret spot. Like she knew it all along.

– Maybe she was looking out for it too. Maybe if she took it she's keeping it safe.

– Rather the ick-it took it.

Effie shivered; she hated when Jr. mentioned the ick-it, that ugly story Ma used to tell them at night from the myth books. It made her neck itch to think of it living under the house like that, and Jr.'s ugly visions of a monstrous old woman wrapped in twigs and roots and muddy rags; how it'd snap out with its long fingers and get you if you didn't go to sleep. First that's all it was, just a story. Just a game. But lately she could tell when he talked about it how Jr. thought the ick-it was real.

– Your foot ok.

– Fine I guess. Thanks for getting Ma.

Effie smiled. She loosened her grip on the book.

– Still wish Ma didn't know the hiding spot though.

Effie felt bad about that too, but at least now maybe Jr. knows why I did it, she thought. She was about to figure out a way to tell him her earlier feeling again, but Jr. bolted to the window.

– Evan!

From the second floor, Evan looked a little gray bug crawling over the hill. His hair was flying around in the wind. Effie couldn't tell but it looked like he had something in his hands—something he was holding tight to make sure the wind wouldn't take it. He crossed the street without looking (she'd remember that next time he took her to the park, told her to check both ways) then he turned the corner towards the house. He walked straight and quick, without slowing down. Soon he disappeared under the lip of the wraparound porch; they listened for the old door to swing in, for the whistle of the wind, the creak of his boots on the wood.

Evan shouldered shut the door against the wind, making sure the deadbolt was in place since the handle lock still jammed. One of these days he'd have to get that fixed. The entryway was dark except for the candlelight pooling down from the iconostasion upstairs—that wall-mounted altar of wooden icons, candles, incense and coins necessary in any Greek household. His own mother had prayed there every morning and every night since he could remember, and Eleni had taken to it too, ever since. He knew if the candles were lit that meant Thea was still asleep so he didn't announce himself.

He sidestepped the stairwell and ducked through the shutter doors separating the landing from a little foyer. He'd barely made it into the room before Kitchen spilled herself between his legs, always the first one to greet him no matter where in the house she'd been hiding before he walked in. His hands were full and he knew she wanted him to rub her ears. It was all he could do to offer a soft Hi, sweet thing before trudging through the room. He felt he knew, somehow, that Kitchen was lonelier here than she'd been in their old compartment back in Johnson City. But it's ok Kitch, he was thinking, I'm home now. At least now maybe she would eat. The walk had made him sweat and he wanted to chuck his coat, but the tight room was officially packed. We've accumulated too much, he thought. Only two years ago now but still all this clutter. It was packed enough as it was when we got here, what with all of Thea's furniture—old armchairs crammed in the corner around the dusted glass end-table, the wide sofa handed down from somebody's cousin, still covered in plastic, not to mention the family photos, the glass armoire lined with what few pieces of china Thea and Mother had retained from their mother's old stint as a neighborhood Avon lady. Evan hated to look at the knickknacks especially—at the metal candleholders and porcelain swans whose beaks he had broken as a boy, all gathering in some silent flock, forcing him to remember. There was too much in this house, they all knew. Not even any room on the cot what with all the laundry. She must have done it all today, he thought, even though I told her not to worry, even though she hates to go down in the basement. He clutched his thin satchel between his knees as he quickly peeled off the gloves, the coat, the sweater underneath, hesitant even to set it down for fear it might melt away into loose socks and paper boxes. Because of the walk his palms had gotten sticky too. He would have to go say hello soon. The house was musky with garlic salt and thyme. He knew that she had put it there.

From their makeshift bedroom Evan made it back through the shutter door and past the stairwell into the kitchen. There she was, his younger half, how he usually found her—a frizzy little thing against the window, checking the pots as if trying to figure how to put them out.

– Smells good, Ellie.

She turned so quickly that she shook her bun loose from its tie.

– Christ Evan what took you.

Evan set his satchel down on the table in the corner. She hadn't set it yet; still there were scattered scraps of paper where she'd scrawled out a chorus of Eleni's in different scripts with a pencil, a little house adrift on a cloud.

– Here lemme move all that. Been a long time now, waiting on you.

– I got it El, don't worry. What's cooking.

Eleni stood rooted between the table and the stove, eyeing Evan's brief.

– Smells like spaghetti. Thea help you with the sauce or—.

– Is it ok, Ev.

– I'm sure it's delicious.

– Evan.

– Come on can't you wait til we eat, I wanna tell everyone together.

– I just think—.

– Well I think you need a drink. Come on Ellie loosen up a little, you want some wine? Still got a couple bottles on the rack.

She moved back to the stovetop, dimming the flame to low, while Evan pulled two coffee mugs and a bottle of red from the cabinet.

– Y'know I been a nervous wreck all day waiting for you to come back. I just wanna know what's the big deal you had to call me in a fuss all the way from Johnson City to—.

– Ellie I promise its good news, just come sit with me a sec huh. Can you come sit with your big brother a minute. I opened one a the blends, oughta go good with the spaghetti. A blend alright with you.

She refastened her bun, came to sit beside him at the table.

– Which mug you want.

– Big one.

– Atta girl.

Evan poured them both a big mug, glad that certain things about his sister had never really changed. There was his frantic little goat, leaping at every crooked floorboard or passing cloud, but there was also a girl here in this room, a mug of red wine in her fingers, caring always too much about it all.

– That sauce smells good y'know.

– It's not spaghetti. There's fasoulakia in the pot.

– You didn't need to go and do all that.

– Well, you're welcome anyway. Cheers.

They clinked mugs, and for a second Evan saw his sister smile. Then she cut her eyes out the window, towards the street.

– What now.

– Oh nothing, just looking at the—. You didn't think to check the mail, did you.

– I sure didn't, but I can. You expecting something.

– No no, it's fine. Better not anyway, case that loon decides to come back.

– What loon.

– That big old loon crouched by the mailbox day in and day out. You'd of seen it if you bothered to look.

– If you say so.

– Well I guess it finally quit. Til tomorrow anyway.

– You sure it was a loon.

– Evan it was a great big old loon crouched right there by the mailbox with its awful red eyes looking like it had a mind to spear the house.

– Come on now, couldn've been any loon. That's a water bird.

– Well, I figured it'd come too far from the lake. But you're not the one watching it look at you through the window every day.

– No I believe you about the bird Ellie, I'm just saying it couldn've been any loon cause loons are waterfowl. Northern birds. Not the best flyers either. Had to of been some crazy loon to end up all the way down here in Comona.

– Well.

They sipped their wine. Eleni watched her mug, Evan watched his sister. Two years already they'd been in this house. And both of them going on thirty-five this June. But his sister looked tired, he could tell. With her hair up in that bun and that flat blue blouse draped over her chest she almost looked just like Ma, only thinner somehow. He wondered if she'd look up at him right now what would she see. He set his mug down, stood up from his seat.

– Lemme set the table.

– Watch out for Jr.'s boot. He got himself stuck in the tree.

– How are the munchkins anyway.

She kept drinking her wine. A truck ambled by out the window, then faded off. Evan returned from the cabinet with six plates which he began to distribute in silence. Eleni looked up from her mug but he wouldn't let her catch his eye.

– Ev.

– Mm.

– It's just us tonight.

– Well, I was talking to Josiah earlier on the phone—.

– Evan.

– He doesn't have work tomorrow so I just told him if he wants he could stop by.

– Why.

– Ellie it's Saturday night. Just for dinner, a drink or two. Don't be like that.

Eleni watched her brother fumble with the silver like trying to keep a wriggling fish in his fingers. She saw his thick curls fall in front of his eyes and she saw him leave them there. This wasn't Evan's way—always so collected even in his most excited moments; he was always so composed. An image came to her then of watching him in Sunday School, flipping through the hymnals in the basement of the church, when she wondered if there wasn't secretly another him living inside his head, piloting his body where it was safe with better controls. But this is also my brother, she noticed, this is also my twin—this bony hand always smoothing out the sheet, even if the fingers tremble. She sighed and took the silver from him, continued placing it.

– Ev. You know I don't care. I like Josiah, really I do. So do the kids. But you know how Thea gets when you bring him around.

– He's not some boy I bring around.

– I know that.

– That's not fair.

– I know that. I think Thea does too but. . .this is her house now. . .that's just the way she is, Ev. All of em, that whole—.

She waved her hand as if it might explain.

When she dropped the last setting on the table and moved to grab his satchel

Evan didn't stop her. She thought for a minute how he must feel—hopping a bus to Johnson City every morning for work only to ride all the way back to this damp intersection, this quiet little olive house of theirs at 108 Park Place, Comona Tennessee, where nothing so terrible or wonderful ever seemed to happen. It was good for him to have another person, she thought. It was good for him to know someone.

– I'll sleep in your study tonight, Ev. Take the bed. If Josiah stays over, I mean.

– You don't have to do that.

– I'm taking the good pillow.

– That's fair.

– One thing.

– Anything.

– You wake up Thea. Get the kids too. Everything's set.

– You got it.

– And Ev.

– Hm.

– Tell em you can't be doing Saturdays anymore. They're working you too hard.

Evan kissed his sister on the temple and strode out to the staircase. Outside a small rain was welling up, the sound like little seeds dropping into the gutters. Evan climbed the staircase slowly now, something misting in his mind. Not sure if it's my shirt that smells or if it's me, he thought. Or maybe it's this house, the rain, these candles, the icona a glimmering pool of sun. Here before these relics a fish was drawn up from his mind—there is someone on the way for me, he thought. There is an organ inside my chest.

From the kitchen his sister called for him again, but he couldn't hear her.

Eleni thought vaguely about the bundle in her hands and wondered about the news—what could he have brought home with him that was so urgent; could it possibly move them, even in a small way, one step further in some direction. I could open it right now to find out, but that wouldn't be right. Besides now it's not the time. The beans are done and surely the twins are hungry too. He'll out with the good news when he wants to. So if Josiah gets to hear it too then all the better. It can wait til we eat.

But outside the window was darkening blue; she hoped if he was coming it would be soon.

Quiet    the light coming down
off the mountain before spreading its blue
across the pavement.    In the cul-de-sac
where Park Place empties itself of its homes
into weed thickets between the neighborhood  &
the highway    there are three children stomping away
from their bikes.    They left
the wheels still spinning.    The light crawls backwards
into the ribs of the mountain    where the Blue Ridge shoulders
its own neighborhood of smoke.

.II.

But it's alright every now and again, Eleni thought as she watched her children scooping icecream from their cups. It's useless anyway, getting Jr. to eat all his beans. Tried all the old tricks too—challenged him to a race, bet him he couldn't finish his plate before me, but our little games don't work as well as they used to. Besides, whatever Jr. does Effie does too, once she knows its ok. So they hardly ate their beans and now they're having icecream and even though they'd be hungry again before long I guess it's alright every now and again. Besides, tonight was supposed to be special. Evan opened another bottle after all. Let him pour me a fresh mug, even. So if the kids want something sweet then why shouldn't they have it. Jr.'s making a mess of himself too, little splatters of vanilla bean streaked across his flannel. Least he behaved when Thea was at the table. Now she's gone back to bed somehow the air's lighter, like closing up a hot oven. But still.

*I'm taking that bookkeeping position at the firm,* Evan had said, *the office handling the newspaper's finances.* Had all the paperwork ready in his brief and everything. Truthfully Eleni expected to feel happier; happier for him but happier also for herself. She trusted Evan to make it work but somehow she thought the news might be better. He'd called her in a fuss all the way from Johnson City, after all. She fixed him his favorite, too. Thea had only nodded her great head. Yes, she seemed to say, what else. Though she didn't say anything at all.

It was a relief though, wasn't it—to sit at the table with her brother, her babies, even Josiah, all sharing a small moment, unclenched. Eleni had settled deep into her chair now, sealed tight in a transparent envelope of her own making. She was still there with the others, but from a distance, like a drawing tacked up on the fridge, more a fixture of the room than an occupant. The twins were contained in their own envelope too, enjoying their treat, making exchanges that only children could understand. Across the table Evan chuckled glossyeyed, his hand on Josiah's knee. Kitchen made herself known under the table, brushing ankles with her long black tail—so very like a cat, always present but never really there. It's good to be together like this, Eleni thought, it really is. But also she was grateful for the protection of her envelope; for not feeling like she had to speak. Whenever she found herself in these moods, safe as a small bird on a sturdy branch, she wondered why couldn't life be like this more often. Anyway it was really too good of Josiah to bring icecream from the Foodland for the twins. He didn't need to do all that, she thought, watching Effie tip the cup back to get the melted trickles at the bottom. But he did bring them something; he always does and now because of him at least they can have something to celebrate with too. Josiah really is a sweet thing, isn't he, even if he's a bit too young for Evan; ten whole years younger than us both and still only in his twenties. A little awkward even, too tall for the grocery's uniform, too slender to fill out the white coat, the wide collar. How he managed to get the job with all that silver in his ears I'll never know. But that's not fair is it. No, that's not for me to decide. Besides, the twins loved him. They'd be asking to go to the park tomorrow, I just know it. I'll be asleep in Evan's study and wake early before Thea to make eggs and toast with peanut butter for the twins and then they'll scurry down to see Evan slouched right here in his thick socks most likely with Josiah wearing one of his shirts and sure enough they'll ask him to take them to the park. That's alright though, I'll have to clean this kitchen sometime. Let them go to the park. Let them enjoy it if it's warm out. Summer will come soon enough.

The pang of Jr.'s cup against the tile snapped Eleni out of her stream like a fish on the line. Luckily he didn't break it, she thought as she rose to grab something to clean with. But Josiah had stood up already; had broken away from Evan's arm to bend down and pick up the cup. Some of the melted icecream had splotched his pantleg but he didn't seem to notice. Instead he just crouched at Jr.'s side telling him not to worry, there's more where that came from. But Eleni took the cup away to the sink. There again, he didn't need to do that. Some suspicious voice inside her murmured it was all for show to keep impressing her in front of Evan, but she knew that wasn't fair either. Maybe some folks are just alright. Really I should be grateful.

– Thank you Josiah, Eleni said. But I think that's all the icecream they need tonight. Jr. did you say thank you to Josiah for bringing you icecream.

Jr. clambered down off his chair and said with his best manners Thank you for the icecream, it was delicious. Effie chimed in not seconds later with her own thank you; she even hugged Josiah's long thigh. That made Eleni proud, to see her children settle into tenderness every now and again, even if it wasn't with her. She was happy to see them behave, especially little Jr., always so rambunctious. She'd let them stay up altogether too late though. They really oughta get to bed soon, she thought, sweeping the rest of the dishes from the table to the sink.

Effie sidled up beside her mother, standing on her toes to reach the sink because her fingers had gotten sticky with the icecream too. Ma stepped aside so she could reach the soap; Effie knew Ma would be proud of her for remembering to use her manners. Always she would tell them both, *If I let you be messy when we're alone then you'll be messy around guests and that's not polite.* But Josiah's not a guest, Effie thought, squelching the suds between her nails; Josiah's just Josiah. He had brought Jr. the treasure for their birthday last summer after all, the one he went to look for today in the secret spot, and that was a nice thing. Nobody else comes over with presents, do they. No, nobody else comes by.

– Alright baby time for you to get to bed, Ma said while twisting off the faucet. Get your brother too, I'll be up to check on you in a while.

Effie went back to push in her chair and saw Jr. still standing by Josiah. He was looking up at him like maybe he wanted him to step in, to say something to Ma about bedtime. But Effie could see too that even Jr. knew that wasn't right. It was a careful way Jr. was looking at him—a way she would never do cause Ma said it wasn't nice to stare like that. But before anything could happen Ma came to kiss them both on the heads and push them off towards the foyer saying Tell the boys goodnight, you'll see them in the morning.

Jr. took the lead out the kitchen onto the floorboards in the foyer, taking his too-big steps that he always did when he wanted Effie to follow him somewhere. They curled their way up the staircase and sat at the landing at the top, draping their legs between the wooden posts of the banister—this, their unspoken secret spot when Ma sent them to bed too early. From here the foyer was like a big ear, echoing all the talk from anywhere else in the house. The light of the icona at the corner of the landing washed the little hallway a deep orange, spilling down across the staircase wall where the cuckoo clock perched, tocking away. Up here, Jr. used to imagine they had a campfire in a cave, sending Effie off into the dark for firewood to keep them warm. But that game's not as fun anymore now that Effie's not scared of the dark like she was. He would have to think up a new game, so they wouldn't have to go back to sleep.

Downstairs Evan was saying something to Ma. Effie could tell Jr. was trying to listen, but all she could hear was the cuckoo clock going. She could see it on the wall in front of them, only half lit by the icona, the long pinecone weights dropping from the wooden villa into the dark like a fisherman's line at the lake. Evan had told it to her one time, how the weights keep the gears in the clock turning and once they drop all the way the clock goes dead. That's how come it has to be wound, he said, otherwise it won't work. She had seen him do it too—how he pulled the long chains with the heavy pinecones all the way back up nice and slow so the clock made a sound like cards shuffling or a curtain coming open. That was a good sound, Effie thought, without knowing what she meant by it. One day maybe I'll be big enough to keep that wound too.

Before long the words Jr. had been trying to catch fell away in jumbles; the cuckoo clock sunk in a warm bath. They both of them had the feeling, even if they wouldn't bother to tell each other, that the moment was over. Something was different now, they knew. The sounds of that moment fell away and now there were different ones instead—rain on the shingle, dishes and whisper, long footsteps from out the kitchen towards Ma's bedroom in the foyer. And this was the moment they both wanted, what they always hoped they would catch if they sat long enough at the top of those stairs—a moment where things would happen that nobody knew they were watching. From their perch the twins watched Josiah trail around the corner behind Evan, the boys' fingers lashed together like toytrain hitches. They listened for the shutter door's rattle, drawing their faces magnetlike against the banister, eager for something they didn't know, something they weren't supposed to have yet. But then Evan flipped the lampswitch by the bedroom door and all the new light spilling out against the stairwell revealed them up on the landing the way Jr. used to flip over rocks for the slugs underneath.

Jr. was the first to lose the banister, scrambling through the hallway shadows with Effie close on his heels. He peeled off, ducking into a corridor they hardly ever used by the bathroom, where a laundry chute down to the basement had been fitted into the wall. He heard Effie behind him but he didn't wait for her. He slid into the crawlspace behind the open closet, crouched with his knees close to his chest behind a screen of winter coats. Effie's footsteps scurried by, stopped, asked *where did you go*, kept going again. Heat cracked in the radiator pipes. The tapping rain turned to knocking. Jr. waited til time went smudgy—was it one minute, two, an hour—before his breathing went back down. He peeled back the curtain of coats. It's safe now, he thought, now I can go.

Come on, fraidy cat, get outta there. They only saw you a second, but probably they didn't even know it was you. Probably they didn't even notice. If anyone got caught it's Effie. She can't run like I can. She doesn't know where to go. This is a spot not even she knows about, my own secret place without her. Might should've put the treasure back here, no way could the ick-it find it then. Not here, not in my secret cave. Effie used to go get the firewood but she never knew about the tunnels, never knew how far back they went. She'd only follow the light so far, but not me. I'm big without the light, I don't need her firewood, I can make it just like this, out the tunnel I found on my own.

Jr. put his hand on the cool wall, fumbled for his footing in the dark until he remembered the way. The cave was wet and cold like before, only now there wasn't a fire to follow. But still he kept his hand on the wall, let it guide him out from the passage, the stone damp underfoot. He kept walking until the creak of the radiator was far away, until even the knocking rain was washed out. He was going deeper, not towards the entrance at all, he realized, but some other way he didn't know. The path sloped down and the air got colder; somehow he knew he was under the house. There should be a fire here, he thought—even without Effie's wood, Thea always keeps the icona burning. She never lets those candles go out. But where is it. Where are the candles and the pictures of the saints, the ones Ma's always talking to at night. Where's the rain, Josiah saying Evan's name, Ma running water in the kitchen. I should turn back now, or else. I was wrong. I don't know the way. I don't know the way and even if Effie was here not knowing the way either at least we'd not know it together. Where are you Ma, did you know about this place too. Could you hear me if I called. I'm sorry about the icecream, about before. And I'm sorry about the tree. Next time I'll take Effie with me, I swear. Next time she won't be alone up there to worry about me.

But then it's another fork in the way, another long tunnel in the dark. And a little light all the sudden in the distance. But it couldn't of been Ma, could it—she was downstairs washing the dishes. And it couldn't of been Thea, she sleeps all day and all night long. But someone put that light there, that little light saying Follow, follow, you don't know the way. And the cave keeps going, dark and cold, and the light keeps saying Follow, and then finally it opens on another room. A brand new room, a room he'd never seen before. But that's not right is it, Jr. asked himself. How come I don't know this room if I live here. Cause don't we live here now, Ma. Isn't this our house now, even though it was Yiayia's first—. This new room is big and dark. It's a fire going in the wall, and all of Yiayia's rugs hanging. And in the big armchair by the fire, it was an old woman slouched over. She's wrapped in blankets and wet leaves. It's her Ma, the woman from the storybook. The ick-it with three faces, the old witch living underground. Only this time she's in disguise, looks like a regular old woman. I can't really tell cause her head's on her chest. But she smells just like your cooking, Ma. Is she sleeping, just sleeping—or is she dead. Her hands are out and open. She wants for me to come here, I can tell. But is she sleeping, Ma, or is she dead. Her face it's all blurry. I wanna see her but I can't. Can she see me. The fire is loud and there are dogs barking out her mouth. Hungry barking, like a whole pack crying for the same bone. I don't like the cave anymore, Ma. I want to go. But I can't—I can't move my feet. The dogs are just barking barking barking. And look, Ma—there it is, my treasure! It's right there on her lap! I can see it right in front of me, the treasure from my birthday last year, sticky with sap from the willow. But how did she get it, Ma. Did you give it to her. Did you give my treasure to the ick-it. How could you, Ma. How come you took it out the tree when you knew I was looking. It could of got me earlier when I was looking and now it's got me anyway. Just look what you did, Ma. How could you. Why would you. Help me, Ma. Get me out of here. Make the dogs stop barking.

Without the sun    electric lamps on the walk
by the neighborhood fitness center peel
shadows across the turf of an old tennis court.    In the light
wild trees huddle behind the black
fence    old men dressed in dew    pushing up the pavement
crushing their honeysuckles into the sky.

# .III.

Eleni could hear them again, from the kitchen, their winter socks hardly muffling their weight on the old wood. Another time maybe she would scold them, but still it was something to hear their small bodies moving and to know they were together. I hope they stay that way, she thought, squeaking the faucet shut; I hope they keep to each other. She worried sometimes how easy it could be to grow apart. Already she would catch herself trying to listen to them when they played—tried to unmask that secret language of theirs, to approach them tender and open palmed. She saw her children sometimes like stray fawn come out the trees at the park, softfooted, wary of everything. But there's no use for that, she thought, blinking back her worries. There are things you can only wait for.

She drew the blinds from the kitchen window again, letting the blue nightfall mingle with the kitchen's little light. The streetposts outside always looked more like lanterns in this weather, the spring mist clouding everything in a soft gauze. But both lights mingled now to spill a thin reflection of her face across the window, making her part of it all—part of the dim kitchen and the checkered table and dark hallways, but part also of the damp earth outside, the cold thickness of March vapor drifting up off the lake. In the window she was all of this together somehow—was cheekbones and curling brow, drooping phonelines, shoescuffed tile, the mailbox gleaming in electric dew. That check's gotta be here soon, she thought with her hands elbow-deep in the dishsoap. Just the trucks running slow, that's all. Just the bad weather coming. Fanny promised she would send it even though I told her we would be fine. But she insisted and after all it's coming all the way from down in Easton by the river. Got to come all the way up and around the mountains. Course it'll take a while, just give it a minute to show. It'll come. Maybe I'll check it tomorrow.

After seeing to it that the lights were all out and the front door double-checked Eleni wrapped her way around the handrail, headed upstairs to Evan's study. From her bedroom a thin light was spilling onto the wood—the warm orange of the floorlamp, she knew. She wished for the starkness of the overhead instead, so she wouldn't feel bad about knocking on the door; she'd forgotten to snag the good pillow. But it's alright, she thought again, it's good for him to have someone. As she mounted the landing she paused by the icona to quickly cast her evening prayers. This she did every night, before the little wooden icons of the saints. But she couldn't concentrate. When she closed her eyes all she could hear was a voice floating through the hallway. She tried to pin it down, and then she was sure—it was Thea.

The doorway to her bedroom was just down the hall, by the staircase leading up to the turret. The twins' bedroom beyond, by the study. It had been her mother's room until last year, until the funeral. Now Thea had claimed it as her own. Most days she kept herself quiet, wrapped up in the room, only coming out to bless the house on Sundays or to eat. With all the pain her hip was giving her, not to mention all that medication, Thea could hardly say a word. But Eleni heard her now clear as ever, talking in a hard voice to the room just as sure as somebody else were in there beside her. Doesn't matter, she was hollering in that same island dialect which Eleni only half-understood, you never listen to me anyhow. You the one who laid down. Don't give me that horseshit, Evi. I don't wanna hear nothing. You the one that left me here. And then you daughter come here with that man like she queen of the castle and she forget the way a jackass smells until he leaves her here too. But let me tell you something—a jackass still a jackass, even if the Father's a horse. *Patera*, she said, using that word which signified the Lord, not simply *baba*. Why you still come by, Thea choked. You gonna burn holes in the carpet, Evi. If you gonna lie down, lie down.

Eleni was staring at a chip of paint on some saint's shoulder. In the red votives on the small chest-of-drawers beneath the candles, a handful of dusted palm leaves were arranged—palms from last year's Sunday. They had all been able to go together, the five of them, last year. And hearing Thea now in that bedroom, speaking to Eleni's mother like she stood just across that threshold, forced her to remember it all—how it was the first Palm Sunday without Mother around; how it was only a week before Easter that year that the church's organ would catch fire in the loft above the narthex and how it had been a warm breeze that year. Thea made it known in her quiet way we all oughta go to the service, Eleni thought, cause that's what you would have wanted. And anyway, she was right; there were so many things you'd still want for us to do, isn't that right Mother. And hadn't the Palm Sunday service always been your favorite—I know you loved listening to the readings, how the Lord came through the Holy Land on an ass' back and all the people had strewn his path with palm leaves cut from the high branches, a symbol of their desire to welcome him, of their desire to see for themselves this miracleworker and the very real desire they had to believe it was all possible somehow. I see you now too, Mother, listening, leaning in the arms of those wooden pews, a woman cut from glittering stone, rooted to the tile, intoning your prayers in that same rasp all the women from the village had inherited. But look at me now, standing here with my hands together staring at the wall, listening to your sister curse you just as sure as if you could hear her; and maybe you can. Can you hear her, Mother; can you hear me too; answer me then, what have I inherited—these little wooden plaques, these sooty votives gathering years of candlewax, parched palms, cotton balls of holy oil spoiling the wood, all these mismatched relics of you and Thea right here in this one corner. And how come I got to look at it every day, Mother. There are drawers I'll never be able to open, did you know that. Whole phials of blessed water just squirreled away behind the leaflets cause you drank out of them, Mother, and that makes them more sacred than any priest's fingertips. And you'll never come back to taste them again. And here I am, standing where all my women have stood before and maybe only cause we felt we should. But I can't stand it, Mother. I can't listen to her anymore. I can't listen to her holler at you like that.

*Glory to you, o God, the Father Almighty, glory to you*—Eleni began when a heavy sound from the bedroom downstairs shook the wood. She cut a quick look to the shutter doors, wondering was this something that needed her attention too, before coming back to the icona, locking eyes with the effigy of St. Helen, her namesake, Equal to the Apostles—*Glory to you, o God, the Father Almighty, glory to you.*

Evan caught himself swearing into Josiah's mouth when he knocked the nightstand over—he'd misjudged how close it was to the cot when he crawled atop the boy's lap. Now the whole movement was spoiled, he thought, untangling his legs from Josiah's; now the whole thing's interrupted. Evan slunk out the sheets to go gather up the mess he made, conscious of himself crouched naked on the floor. He snatched the items up in a frenzy, the whole time thinking only how the curve of his back might look to Josiah from the bed. How would he notice the weathered ribcage, the steppingstone spine; did his thighs, once muscular and sturdy, still seem new, or did the shadows from the lamp only highlight the sheer skin sure to wrinkle soon, all the hair rubbed clean from years of cycling friction; did his balls droop too low to the carpet in some way that might suggest he was no longer a fresh twentysomething looking for god knows what in the shaded bathroom bars and secret porches of his younger summers? There on the floor, with a pile of his sister's things, Evan could feel the hardness between his legs begin to soften as the warmth was drained away. Stop thinking about it, he chided himself, you'll only make it worse. But really of all the things to happen this somehow seemed fitting. It was supposed to be a special day after all and here I am picking up postcards and elastic off the floor when I oughta be in bed with this boy who's laughing now when he oughta be touching me; laughing cause that's what folks do in a situation to diffuse it, they laugh it off; any gracious person would, anyway. But now the whole thing's gotta start all over again, he thought, standing up to right the nightstand. But I'm not sure I've even got it in me to start it up again, he was thinking, when Josiah said—

– Hey, you.

It's the way he said it made Evan look him in the eyes; that same easy way about him snagged his attention in the first place. It was a way that said I see you and

I want you and I've never seen you before all at once. Evan leaned into the mattress but didn't get in, eyeing Josiah for the first time all over again. There's no way, he thought, that this is mine, overwhelmed by the ease of Josiah's movements—the careless way he cocked one knee up in the air and the other leg sprawled straight out, not caring or maybe not noticing how his balls flapped across his long thigh, like his own body simply hadn't occurred to him in some way. Evan felt himself tense, eager to rediscover that body stretched out and waiting for him. There's just no way, he kept thinking, as he blinked against the little chinks of lamplight coming off Josiah's piercings. The silver in his soft lobes and smooth cartilage, it all seemed pressed into him since birth by some strange design. He was a temple himself, this boy—those same collarbones he'd once found shelter in jutting now like steel rafters in the plastic film of a new building; the nectarine fuzz of his shoulders stitched into with bright tattoo, the blues and silver hues of ocean ink casting waves with every raise of arm. What did I do, Evan wondered, setting one knee back on the mattress, to deserve this fresh young thing. My fruit's already flowered and fallen, but still two years and here comes the same hand reaching—fingers which have known the depth of me and want to know them still; here comes a mouth that says *come here* on every opening and hands that help me back into the bed; hands hitched to long arms wrapped around these hairless thighs cupping half of me in each palm; hands that I know can keep me. But for how long, he tried not to wonder, the warmth flowing back in again—how long can I keep this to me, pressed closer than his hand on my back, or my cock on the smooth banks of his naval. I've seen these eyes before, I oughta know. I've seen skin crawl away on its own. There have been boys on my beaches, windswept heroes of some island fantasy scrawled out in the dark and all of them sculpted to rubble; years of men reduced to broken debris bobbing up out of the foam. There was the Italian who always tugged at my teeth, the Father's son with fisherman hands and the fisherman who sucked all his secrets from my earlobe. But they've all swashed away now, sunk in a faraway whorl of salt and pebble. But here now is a boy who never once asked about all that; who peels my flesh back with precision, his careful fingers lost in the damp hollows, our cocks blooming together like gardenia after nights of warm rain. There is room enough inside of me, somehow, even for him. How strange that this jaw fits in my hand and that some tender part of me is safe in this jaw; how entirely unreal at all that there are parts of us both still open enough to receive each other.

– C'mere, Josiah said as he laid back on the pillow, guiding Evan's waist toward his lips. He could tell Evan was unsure; felt him tremble as his fingers found that soft bramble of hair between his thighs, the clench of his muscles contracting those old worries—am I good, is it clean, are you sure. But of course I am, Josiah said without saying; of course you are. He clutched Evan's hipbones tighter, a gentle affirmation that yes, I want you, even when you tremble and yes, you are a body with your own taste and yes, I like that. Josiah turned his man around, guided the smooth thighs to his lips, sustaining the weight of the body above him; he let the warm flesh open up and drape across his face as he inhaled the unwrapped skin, hot with wanting and uncertainty. I know he is worried, Josiah thought, unfolding his tongue, but this is how I can show him I'm here. I know he is worried about getting older and me barely twenty-five. I know he is worried about his job, his sister, the twins, and I know also he is worried about making too much noise in this quiet little olive house that doesn't even belong to him but belongs to his dead mother's sister. I know. I know he is worried about it all and I want to make it easier for him, true, but I also never want to have him unless it's like this—mixing his smell with my smell, his taste on my cheeks, the heat of him open and me knowing that it's me who he's opening for. Just take as long as he needs to relax and then take a little longer still, the cramp of my jaw worth every cracking of his toes, the catch of air in his throat, this little language of labor we speak to remind each other that yes, you are good and yes, I am sure and yes, I want only you.

Afterwards, when the heat had spilled out of them both into the other and the towels were tossed to the floor, Evan held Josiah in the crook of his arm, thumbing one of his earrings.

– That was sweet of you earlier. Bringing icecream for the twins.

– It's nothing. You know I love em too.

– I know, but still. You made their night.

Josiah nipped at Evan's nipple with his teeth.

– Careful.

– Is that the only night I made.

I miss that energy, Evan started to think, that always being ready for another round of anything, no matter what it was. Nothing stops the wanting to though, not really. Just after a while you get tired is all. But where's it all go, he wondered. Just beyond the scrolling doors he could hear Kitchen mewling against the tracks, her knowing that he was inside and wanting to be with him too. He wondered how long she'd been waiting, sorry for having to keep her separate from this showing of love. I will have to let her in at some point.

– We should get to sleep. They'll want to see you again in the morning.

– I'll be around.

– You don't have plans.

– Not really. Told my ma I'd drop back by later on. Gotta help her with the T.V. again. She's useless with that stuff.

– They'll wear you out, you know.

– I don't mind.

– If you say so.

– I say so.

– Alright.

– Hey.

– Hey.

– What's up.

– What do you mean what's up.

– Come on now, don't do that. What's on your mind.

– Nothing. Nothing, really. It's—.

– Your sister.

–

– She tries, you know.

–

– Evan.

– Yeah.

– You don't think so.

– It's not that.

– What then.

– Just her, the way she is. I don't know. It's been hard on her, especially after, well, you know. With the twins and all.

– Their father.

– Mhm.

– Real shit of him.

– Yeah. Bad timing.

– Is there ever a good time to get left.

– No, but. This was—. It was right when Mother started to get, you know.

– Oh.

– Three whole years it took her to go. And now two years later and, you know. I just don't know what I'm still doing in this house. Any of us.

– Well, your aunt. She needs you too.

– It's different.

– How different.

– Thea's stubborn as sin. She's not in any hurry to go. Besides, with her it's just her body. Just that hip is all. Not like Mother. That's—. It's a whole different thing. With Mother it was her mind. The forgetfulness. The accidents. Just the whole of it slipping away.

– Hmmm.

– Besides, I can't keep—.

– What.

– Keep doing this.

– Keep doing what.

– Not you, come on. I don't mean it like that. C'mere. I only mean—. I mean I'm thirty-five years old and now I'm back living in the house I grew up in. Both my folks dead. Driving a town over for work. Answering to a woman who isn't my mother and raising children that aren't my own.

– You don't mean that.

– I don't—. I mean, I don't mean for it to sound that harsh. But still. What am I doing. I just don't know what I'm doing here.

– You're doing just fine.

Evan fumbled with the ring in Josiah's ear, spinning it between his fingers. This must be just as strange for him, he thought, this sneaking away, even when you carry it with you all the same. Evan hadn't worn jewelry in years, had stopped wearing his own cross years ago—the one his mother brought back for him from the island. Why is it that still we have to deal our love this way, in the shadow of our mothers' religion. Why is it, he wondered, that—. Out in the hall the cuckoo clock started going, the swing and shut of its villa doors striking the moment in two with their hatchets. He had forgotten he even wound it that morning.

Effie rolled over up in her bed after the fifth caw, still wide awake. She lost count how many cuckoos it made but she knew it was too many; she knew she oughta be asleep.

Beside her, Jr. was a fuzzy heap in the streetlight coming through the windows. He'd shot into the room just behind her, after they got split up on the balcony, and went straight to bed without a word, shut tight underneath the covers. She tried to reach out to him in that quiet way they could do sometimes, try to see if he was awake without saying something. But she would of felt bad if he wasn't and she woke him. Her stomach grumbled and she looked across the room so she wouldn't have to think about it. There was the bookcase with her brother's toys on top, the curtains breathing in the little draft; there were the speckles on the ceiling which she thought one day maybe she would count if only she had enough time. None of these could help her though, she knew. Giant squids still loomed outside the window, but she knew they weren't real. Not like that icky feeling from before, about Jr. being gone; that was a real feeling; that was something not right. Ma used to tell it to them both how Effie came out a few minutes before Jr. which is the opposite of how it was with Evan and Ma. The way Ma told it, Effie was crying so hard when she came and didn't stop til Jr. was out too. That made Effie wonder sometimes how she ever managed those first few minutes without him. She was glad she couldn't remember.

She wouldn't know it, but Jr. was awake in his bed beside her, grinding his teeth about the stolen treasure, wondering how long it would take for the ick-it to come looking for him too.

It was a small spell    the rain dripping
little mirrors into potholes on the pavement.    Now &
again a streak of pickup trucks come sweeping away
water on the highway.    Somewhere off behind the trees
the low thunder of a freight train on its way east
to the Carolinas.    Just the new moon's silver hangnail
in the sky's blue bowl    even the clouds gone to rest.

# .IV.

The loon had come back.

All morning it circled the reaches of the lake, diving into the dark in search of something to spear. Its eyes seared the banks where the water lapped up unfamiliar pieces onto the reeds—those same banks where the loon might have raised its young had they survived the winter or the propeller boats or the stray brambles snagging them undercurrent by their little wings. But now it had been fed, returning to caw its throat out in the mist, in that same patch of grass beside the olive house, the scales of some unlucky trout still sticking to its bill. The blue was only just now happening and already it had found itself a meal. Now all there was to do was wait. It would have to lay a new clutch before long, it knew, just as soon as its mate returned. The eye drew the house in, reassuring that yes, this is the place it had claimed. The loon puffed its breast feathers at the version of itself reflected in the windows' early light, not recognizing threat from familiar. In an upstairs window, above the hanging lip of the wraparound porch, an orange light came on to break the morning blue.

She'd have to wash the sheets again, there was no way around it, even though she'd done a load yesterday. Jr. never did wet the bed, least not since he was a tiny thing, Eleni thought while she rocked him against her breast, so why's it happening now? Before she heard him she'd been caught in one of her dreams again, only she couldn't remember it clear. Had it been one of the usual, the recurring ones she never seemed to shake, it might not have bothered her so much. But it was something about this one made her feel like she might not even be awake right now. Something about a house, a little log cabin floating downstream between the mountains, only instead of water it was a stream of brown dirt and green earth, white tombstones bobbing up out the froth like stones. Too early for all this, she thought, rubbing Jr.'s back with her palm. What is it baby, she kept asking him, but all he could say was—

– She took it Ma, she took it, I know she did.

– It's ok, *Strataki-mou*, you're alright, it's just us now.

– But she took it, I know she took it.

– Nobody took nothing baby.

– Then you gave it to her.

– Gave it to who.

– You can't see her now, she's hiding.

– Hiding in this house, no such thing.

– Is too, I see her, I know she's here.

– Who do you see, Strati.

– Why'd you give it to her, Ma.

– Not nobody else around but us, now.

– Don't you know she's coming to get me too.

– Efstratios that's enough, now who did you see in this house.

– The ick-it!

Eleni hadn't noticed she'd screwed Jr.'s shirt into a tight ball until her fingernails started to dig at his shoulder. When he jolted under the pinch she loosened her grip, looking not for or at anything but in the direction of the curtained window. She hadn't expected this yesterday, when she hollered at him for playing in the tree. Cause it was her fault, wasn't it, rattling them like that. Telling them scary stories to get them to sleep, to leave her alone for one minute out the day. But no, they just don't understand how small they are, and if I don't remind them who will. Besides, they get like this too often, so invested in their own games. With Jr.'s little head pressed against her breast she worried she might never really understand what went on in there.

– Come on now Jr., let's go downstairs. I'll make us some chai. You want to have some chai with Ma.

Jr. nodded his head.

– Alright, let's go. Be quiet now, we don't want to wake anyone else up. You know your Thea's still sleeping.

Effie was listening the whole time in her own bed. Even before Ma came in the room she knew Jr. was upset. She could feel it before he even started to cry. Course she wanted to say something to him to help but nothing seemed like the right thing. Truth be told she was afraid too. Afraid maybe that what if Jr. was right the whole time about the ick-it. Now she didn't know anymore how many of the games they used to play were games and how many maybe were real. She was listening now to their feet going down the hallway, away from her. She could smell the stain Jr. had made, trying not to think of what the sheets looked like, dark and mushy. And she hated to think of Jr. like that, of something like that happening to him. I oughta go see him, Effie thought. He's my little brother and he's always making sure about me so I should go down to make sure about him too. That's what Evan does for Ma after all. So that's what I should do.

Downstairs, Evan was the first to dress and leave the room. He was sure he'd heard someone coming down the staircase crying. Josiah he kissed between the shoulderblades and left him to sleep a little longer before throwing on a pair of boxers, a longsleeved knit shirt. He found them in the kitchen, his sister at the stove with a waterpot, Jr. in a chair with his chin on the table.

– Morning.

– Oh god, Evan.

– Whatsa matter sis.

Eleni didn't answer him. Jr. just stared at the fridge.

– How you feeling big guy.

Evan sat beside him, tousling his curls with his fingers.

– Bad dreams, he asked his sister.

– We had a little accident.

– Oh.

– Mhm.

– Hmm.

– Yep.

– Well that's alright big guy, the bad dreams are gone now.

– It's not a dream, it's the ick-it.

– Jr. what did I tell you.

– The ick-it huh, didn't know we had an ick-it.

– Evan don't encourage him.

– But you listen here buddy, it's gone now, alright, no more tears.

– Evan.

Evan cut his sister a look that said *just let me handle this one* and she turned herself back to the tea.

– Tell you what, how about let's get out the house today. How about we go to the park. You know Josiah still thinks he can beat you in a race, can you believe it.

Jr. mumbled something as the kettle started to whine.

– What's that bud.

– I said well he can't. He'll never beat me. Josiah's too slow.

– That's what I keep telling him. He won't listen to me. You gotta be the one to remind him, alright.

Jr. nodded. Eleni pinched a mix of tea into the diffuser.

– Atta boy.

– Here you go baby, Eleni said. Just let it steep a minute or two.

Eleni cranked the stove back down, moved the kettle to a different eye. Still it bubbled out its steam into the room. Outside the loon kept cawing against the morning birds. From upstairs quick footsteps fumbled down the hall while the shutter door opened again. After a muffled moment Effie and Josiah emerged from the entryway, her arm around his slender thigh.

– Speak of the devil and she shall appear. Just telling Jr. here you're outta your head if you still think you can beat him in a race. What do you think Effie, I say we do a rematch today in the park. I mean, if Josiah's up to the challenge.

Eleni held the warm mug up to her temples. She was grateful, but still annoyed to see Evan trying so hard like this. He shouldn't have to do that, she thought, keeping it all together first thing in the morning when he hasn't even gotten up yet. But neither should I, she started before biting her cheeks at the thought. Of course you deserve it, you're their mother after all. If not you then who else? Still, Evan always was better at this; acted more like they were his very own two children in a way their father never did, the bastard. But no, absolutely not, I will not let that man into my head today and certainly not this early. She pressed the mug harder into her temple; some of the tea sloshed out onto her forearm but she didn't move to temper the burn with a palm. Let it hurt a little, she thought. Let it burn him out my mind.

*So anyway* Evan was saying to the twins, though she only halfway heard him. Josiah had taken Effie's curls into his palm, guiding her towards the stairs. Evan scooped Jr. up into his arms despite how big he'd gotten. Eleni watched the movement through a film of salt, thinking the whole time, I oughta say something, do something, offer the boys some coffee at least, offer to pack some fruit in a baggie, anything but let them just scoop up my children and carry them away for the day cause they know I can't handle them myself. But it would be fine, the boys would take care. They would take better care than I could and even though they don't mean it that way that's what we all know. Besides, this whole morning's my fault. I could just kick myself for ever telling the twins those stories in the first place; could just absolutely wring my own neck. I'd only meant it as a story after all, when we first moved in, to try and scare them into sleeping; some story from the mythology books my own mother gave me as a child. And didn't Evan and I always love those stories—where titans stole fire from the gods, or gods turned people into salt, or any other ridiculous thing the Greeks made up to try and make some sense out of the world. And who knows what story they latched onto like that anyway, who knows which ghost or god they think they saw. Ick-it, ick-it, old woman under the house—none of that sounded familiar. They always did get too wrapped up in their games. They never go to bed at a decent hour anyway, no matter what I say. So what's it matter, why'd I even bother with those stories; they only run away with it and look now where it's got em. Just look now what you did.

Eleni went back upstairs and pulled the sheets off Jr.'s bed, careful to walk soft past Thea's room even though the boys were laughing loud with the twins downstairs. She balled the sheets up tight and cracked a window for some air. But it wasn't the smell that bothered her. It was the dream. Still she couldn't shake it, couldn't remember just what happened or where the dream dropped off in the real world. As she walked back down the hallway and past the icona, she caught St. Helen by the eyes—her head wrapped in royal maroon, palms upturned, a miniature golden cross hovering between her arms. She thought about saying something, but just made her way back downstairs, past the foyer, where the boys had the twins seated on the cot, helping them with their boots.

Underneath the stairs was a thin wooden door on a latch to the basement. Eleni shifted the bundle of wet cloth to her hip, unhooked the lock slowly. There was that same rickety staircase curving around from a triangular landing into the earth, where the washer and dryer units rested on the concrete floor. Eleni took a step down and scanned the darkness under the house. In the low light, it was all just dusty shapes. Nothing in particular. But it had been everything once, hadn't it—all of Mother's things. *Throw it down*, Eleni heard her mother say from the foot of the stairs, always hollering for her and Evan to bring her their school clothes. *Just throw it down, all the way. I take care of it.* Eleni's arm started twitching. Fine then, she thought, and bunched up the sheets and flung them down towards the machines, you take care of it. She locked the basement door behind her.

It took her some time to realize that the house had been emptied. And the silence was too big. The quiet of the whole house hollering in her ears. She went quick to the kitchen windows, her forearm still twitching, and fumbled until finally they swung open. She inhaled all the noises coming through—a bike in the slush, some truck beeping unseen down the road, even the caw of the loon, still there on the grassy knoll beside the mailbox. She wiped the sweat from her forehead. There at the intersection of Summit and Park her children scurried across the street with the boys—those tiny little frames wrapped tight in their coats looking absolutely miniature in comparison. One of them, she couldn't tell which, strode a bit too confidently into the road without looking before Evan shot out a protective arm. I wouldn't be able to do that, she thought, as they turned the corner south towards the park. I wouldn't be able to help them if they ran. Now they'd passed out from her vision completely, leaving Summit to run its course alone. Their plot on the corner was the last historic house north of Park Place before the street opened up onto the drug store, a filling station, that new complex they'd only just finished building. The few trees behind the big willow out back obscured most of the ugly brick, but still she could hear the occasional television left on, conversations come down from open balconies. For once she welcomed this. Some man was just now calling up to someone he knew from the street.

– Jerry! Jerry, you up yet!

– Who's 'at now.

– Terrence Anderson, up the road.

– Well I'll be, how you doing.

– Alright, alright. How you.

– Oh, you know.

– Mhm.

– Tell me what's good.

– Well, nothing too good.

– That right.

– Mhm.

– Well, come on now.

– You member Hubert Rochelle, come up to Sissy's every now n' again to drink.

– Shore do, fella in the corner always playin' checkers, army man, went by Huby.

– Very same.

– Shore I knew him, don't tell me.

– Well, he died.

– Naw.

– Mhm.

– When.

– Last night.

– Hell.

– I know it.

– That was a good man, Hubert Rochelle.

– I know it.

– What took him.

– Can't say, just heard it from Sissy this mornin'.

– That's a real shame.

– That's what I said.

– Mhm.

– Well listen, you come on by Sissy's sometime, she wants you for a bite.

– Alright, you kiss her for me.

– Will do.

– Alright Terrence.

– Alright.

Eleni had been listening so close that she didn't even hear Thea come down the stairs until she was already at the landing.

It's not right, Sophia Kefalas thought, standing at the kitchen threshold. That girl will spend her whole life looking out the window. No good way to be. She comes with the crying babies and never tells them right. She has to put her hands on them or else they never learn. But she won't. She won't touch them. She won't even brush her hair. First thing in the morning and still she looks a sack of wheat. See now how she pulls it back knowing she forgot. That girl is not aware of herself; still a girl no matter what she thinks she is, a mother only by birth. See now how she moves to clean a spill she thinks I wouldn't see. She hasn't cleaned up after dinner either, dishes still in the sink, the child's boot still muddy by the door. Nothing moved, nothing put back in its place. Not the least bit like her mother.

When Evi was around the floors were always clean. Copper on Saturdays, sweetbread on Sunday mornings. Already after ten o'clock and still she hasn't censed the house. And even after I went to all the trouble of ordering new coals from the Daughters, had Theodora bring them over from across town herself, and now they're just sitting there unwrapped by the icona. The house should always be blessed on Sunday and she knows I can't do it myself. She knows too well about this hip; knows it's not like it used to. Now the willow branches reach long as the devil's shadow, no one there to prune the bushes even, nobody to water the yard. Just you wait til I get the operation, then we'll see who's running this house. No, if Evi were here she would talk some sense into that girl. Evi would remind her whose house. Would remind her what to do. But she should know on her own what to do, or did she forget when she left with that man, that fool from the city with the evil eyes. That's a man you don't let into your house not even if he shit gold. That's a man to stay away from. *Efstratios* he called himself, *the right path*, as if there were any right thing about him. She should listen to the meaning of a name; should think that if it sounds too good it just might be. He wouldn't know the right path from a ditch. But now she sees what clothes a man like that can wear and her little one stuck with the name now too. Now she sees where it gets you, running off like that, unmarried, alone, the children not even properly baptized and their mother a fumbling mess who spends whole days at the window. No, that's no good way to be.

Something she says to me now, too quiet. Something about the mail. She dries her hands on a towel and for a minute she does look just like Evi. That same nervous way they share, ruffling the cloth like trapping a bee, so much energy on the smallest tasks. She could clutch the towel once and be done with it but instead she shakes it like so. Instead she rattles it out. Of course it can't be helped, what your mother leaves behind. After all she is her mother's daughter, but Evi never forgot it either, went too easy on her. Now she leans too heavy on her brother; her own children will do the same; long after they're grown and I'm gone and they take to their own ways they will see how their ways are not so different in the end. The boy will stumble through his own path, never knowing of his father's pit. The girl too will have a window like her mother. They will grow up exactly the same. Look at them and you can see it already, how they will slouch in their old age, how their skin will set with the years, but now too young to even hold the thought. A family like this you can tell already how we will all end up. Evi knew it. Ever since the islands Evi had known, when she looked into the well at Agia Paraskevi and heard the lord's whisper and saw her namesake's reflection in the water she knew. We should have stayed on that island. Evi should have joined the monastery after all; we should have never left the village, no matter had a raid come, or fire fall to the earth, then we ought to have burned on our own soil. But no, that's no more right than what we did, is it. No more noble than running away. See this girl in front of me looking out the window just like her mother and of course it all comes together; Evi had her own window in Cecil. The little girl will have hers too. But these old eyes have had enough of windows gleaming, of hot light, cold winds, the world climbing in on its own. Now she goes past me with the same small voice and when she opens the front door you would have hardly thought a breeze went by. See now this kitchen without her inside; see these counters where my sister carved the tomatoes and skinned the chickens; the stove where she stirred the baklava syrup and that table where she dried wheat for the koliva, calling me *koukla* while I candied the almonds. Where has that sheet gone to, where did I put her pans. This tile has worn us all together. Would it know anymore which one of us walks here; would so much difference be made at that stove, between me or my sister or this daughter of hers now crossing the sidewalk alone, towards the mailbox at the corner. She goes there like her mind is set, like she knows what she means to do. For a moment Evi's courage is with her, I can see. But then the trees must become very big and the houses and the lawn and the bikes running by on the path. Some bird shape flaps its angry wings. It has cried all morning since the spring.

Sophia Kefalas nodded her great head. It stops her where she stands, the world, you can see. She's come to her own well, that girl, but she will never look inside. She will come back. She will come back into the house and always come back. That girl will never make it out.

Couple houses down     the baby blue Queen Anne
revival cracks her window open     shakes her shavings off.     A woman
on the phone inside     howling or laughing under the electric
swash of a blender going.     In the little alley between the garage
&  the Victorian guarding the wrought-iron gate to her garden
an old man scratches his halo with a free hand     the other
letting a match to his cigar.     Overhead     the cirrus gather like guests
at a party still unintroduced  &  back on the blue porch     a dog throws
its bark against the blender     so suddenly covered in shade.
But then the clouds split up again  &  the dog stands     shakes the blue
flakes from its fur     folds its paws back under its chin.

## .V.

– They're doing what now, Eleni was saying to her cousin Fanny over the phone, her neck craned awkwardly against the receiver.

It was only just now past noon and Thea had gone back to her bedroom after all. I knew she wouldn't stay downstairs for long, Eleni thought. Better for it anyway, the house is too tight with her shuffling around. The boys still weren't back with the twins. Probably one of them found something by the lake to play with; Jr. had brought back those fishbones once for fun, didn't he. Hate to think of them out there by the water, full of cold currents just waiting to suck them under, but they were with the boys after all; the boys would take care; the boys always did. Anyway Fanny's check still hadn't come and that loon just wouldn't quit, perched out there morning til night with its hot eyes scanning, watching, defending what it decided it owned. So the best thing for it was just to call Fanny up, Eleni had thought, just to ask her herself what was the matter with the check. At first she didn't feel right making the call since she hadn't asked for the money in the first place, but Fanny had insisted. No, Fanny would take no refusal. *It's just the roads is all, Elenitsa*, Fanny had said, using the village suffix her mother had always latched onto their names when she called them—that extra little bit of familiarity built into the word, a sound Eleni always associated with closeness, comfort, warmth.

*I don't know what else to tell you, Nitsa*, she had been saying, but Eleni could tell she was distracted; she'd been saying something about her own boy, a strange kid living up on the plateau in Middle Tennessee whose name Eleni couldn't remember, running off somewhere with his friends. Naturally Fanny was frazzled, her son living near three hundred miles away and now suddenly disappeared without a trace; he'd passed through Easton by the river sometime that morning, Fanny was saying, but that was the last they'd heard of him.

– Now just what am I supposed to *think*, Nitsa, Fanny crooned across the line.

– I don't know what to tell you, Fanoula.

Eleni meant to be more sympathetic. Of course it was awful, just awful, what Fanny was going through; she could hardly bear the thought of her own babies grown, let alone running off, but she couldn't hide that the missing check was distressing her more. Fanny hadn't even told her how much she'd written it for and at this point it was too late to ask; that wouldn't be polite, no matter were they family or no; that would spoil the whole thing. She shifted the receiver to the other shoulder.

– Last I heard he'd taken some van with his friends from the university, you know that little band they've got together I told you about. Something about noise, I don't remember. Listen Ma, he says to me, we left Middlesboro and we're coming down through Easton this very minute. I said well how come you didn't tell me, I woulda fixed y'all something to eat for when you drop by. I'm clean out, Nitsa, on account of working like I have. Why, I don't think I've been to the store all week. You know how George gets too, always eating out with his clients. I just have me a banana or some cereal and that's my dinner most days. Anyways, I said to him, I don't have a thing in the fridge for when you come—

Eleni supplied the appropriate mhm's and is-that-right's, all the while plucking some loose fiber come unraveled from her jeans. When Fanny got to talking there was no stopping her til she was done. Eleni had enjoyed these conversations more when they were both younger, calling each other up just to remember all those summers they'd spent down in Fanny's hometown, in that scruffy little city by the Tennessee River. Eleni's mother had sworn she'd never return to the islands, not after making it out of there with Thea in tow during the War. So the next best thing had been to send Evan and Eleni down to Easton, so she could work the steakhouse full-time in the summers. The girls would summon those summers different every time, always changing with their little variations—stories and stories of Evan and Eleni's games as children, of Fanny as a child herself, all of them roaming that property tucked up in the mountains while Fanny's parents, Uncle Pat and Aunt Helen (rest their souls), tended to the house. They only came back in pieces, those days, but still Fanny and Eleni felt some ancient obligation to keep it alive. How warm those summers with Fanny had been. But they were both mothers now; had both lost their own mothers too. There was too much to worry in the present now. Fanny must've figured you can't keep pulling up the past forever.

– So then he says to me, Ma, we're not stopping by. I said what do you mean you're not stopping by, of course you're stopping by! This is his very own house after all, the one he grew up in. But he says No, Ma, we're just on our way east over the mountains, no time to pass through. Said something about heading out to Southport, hell if I know where that is. Do you know of any place at all named Southport? I never heard of such a place. Usually I wouldn't think twice about it Nitsa but something in his way wasn't right. I mean something about how he said it to me's got me worried. Course I tried to ask him what it was got into him but he just said, Gotta go Ma, we're hitting a tunnel, then he went and hung up on me. His own mother. That was near two whole hours ago, Nitsa, what am I supposed to think? Elenitsa, you still there? Hello—.

– I'm here Fanoula, sorry.

– Oh. Ok. Everything alright, you don't sound too good.

– It's nothing, Fanoula. Just a headache is all.

– Oh come on *koukla*, what is it. I told you that check oughta get to you soon. If it doesn't come tomorrow I'll call up the postal people myself, then they'll really be in trouble.

– No, no. I mean thank you, Fanoula, it's not—you've done so much already. It's not that. And I know—.

– What is it, tell me.

– You've got enough on your plate already.

– Nitsa I'd shake you through this phone if I could. Come on now, don't be so stubborn. What's on your mind.

– I had a dream.

– Oh, Fanny said across the line, almost in a whisper. I see.

– Mhm.

– A bad one.

– I don't know. I mean, I think so. I can't really remember.

– Hmm.

– I mean I woke up and the kids were screaming and I just—I don't remember really when the dream stopped or what. And it's not that the dream itself was bad, more like I felt bad for coming out the dream.

– Ok. Tell it to me slow, Nitsa. What do you remember. You must remember something.

– I don't know. It was real early. And I think I was asleep. You know how sometimes you wake up but you're not really awake, and you got your eyes still closed and everything. It was like that. And then—.

– And what.

– I was sleeping in Evan's study. He had a—. Anyway, I was on the futon. Nobody else in the room with me. And the kids were still asleep, just right across the hallway. So it couldnt've been anybody.

– What happened, Nitsa.

– Somebody kissed me. I mean I felt a kiss on my cheek. I'm sure I did. Only it was so early, and I didn't have my eyes open.

– You sure you weren't dreaming about *him*.

– No, it didn't feel like him at all. He never kissed me like that. I—I feel so strange even saying it to you now Fanoula but—. I think it was her. I think it was my mother.

Fanny was quiet over the phone. Eleni could hear the chain jingle across the line as she crossed herself.

– I don't know how, Eleni continued, but—.

– Nitsa, listen.

– Fanoula, I know how it sounds. But look, I was—I don't know how to explain it to you, but I just woke up feeling like she was with me.

– She's always gonna be with you, Nitsa. Thea Evi loved you so much, you don't even know. Of course she's with you.

– I know, but—that's not what I mean.

– Eleni listen to me. Your ma was the best. I mean really, just an incredible woman. And she had nothing but love for you and Evan and those babies of yours. Hell, she was like a second mother to me too and we're not even bound by blood. But that's just how she was, Nitsa. She was a good woman. I cried my eyes out when she went. And seeing you and Evan and everyone at that funeral, well, that was one of the hardest things I ever had to see. But she's at peace now, baby. You just have to believe that.

– I just—.

– Oh, baby, it's not easy. And I can't lie and say if it maybe gets easier. Cause who knows if it does or it doesn't. I miss my ma every day. Used to talk to her about my dreams too, same as you. She'd read my coffee grounds and everything, tell me the craziest stories. You know she always used to call me Mrs. Smith even when we were little, and look what happened—I married me a Smith.

– You sure did.

– I sure did.

– Remember the story about the pie.

– That old story, how could I forget.

– Tell it to me again, would you.

– Oh Nitsa, you know it just a good as I do.

– I like it better the way you tell it.

– Well. First of all you remember my mother's cooking. God bless that woman and everything her hands have done but she couldn't whip up a decent meal to save her life. Not like Thea Evi. It's a good thing our fathers were both in the restaurant business otherwise I think we'd have been like to starve. But my ma, she was slick. Always had her eyes out for a deal. And one a those summers when you and Evan had come down, Daddy made us a little barbecue. And for dessert, Ma brings out a pecan pie hot out the oven, with icecream and everything, all the fixins. And Nitsa I wish to god I had a picture of your face when you bit into that pie. It was like you'd tasted heaven. Course you probably never had pecan pie before in your life. Thea Evi was too busy baking y'all sweetbread, baklava, galaktobouriko—all those good Greek sweets she made so well. She absolutely spoiled y'all rotten. But that pecan pie was about the tastiest thing you ever had in your life. And all I remember is after y'all had gone back up to Comona that year your mother she gave my mother a call, said *Eleni mou, what kind sweets you been giving my babies? They want me to make them this pie, some Americaniko thing. Where you get you recipe?* And I was sitting right there at the kitchen table watching my ma just absolutely crack herself up. Cause then she says to your ma, she says *I tell you where I got it, koukla mou, that's a Mrs. Smithopoulous pie from the supermarket.* Can you believe it, a Mrs. Smith brand pie from the Piggly-Wiggly down the road. And it was frozen, too! Ma didn't have to do nothing but pop it in the oven. Truth be told, I'm surprised she didn't burn it. Oh, they laughed and laughed about that for years, Nitsa.

Eleni was laughing now too, despite herself.

– They were angels, our mothers. They really were. And it's not a day goes by I don't wish I could just ring mine up and hear her voice and say Hey Ma, whatcha cookin' tonight. So many things I still wanna tell her. But that doesn't change it, Nitsa. It is what it is.

– I know.

– I'm only saying it cause I love you, Nitsa. Like a sister, you know that. And I don't doubt you had a dream. All I'm saying is it was a dream, baby, that's all. Try to be happy about it. I haven't dreamed about my own mother in years. Guess she got better things to do up there than loose me some sleep.

– You're right.

– I know it. Now you just perk up a little Nitsa, you hear me. I hate to hear you so gloomy all the time. And you call me about that check tomorrow, alright. They don't want me to call em, that'd be all she wrote and you know it.

Afterwards, when the two had said their goodbyes and Fanny promised to light a candle for them both at church next week, Eleni brewed herself another pot of chai, which she took to the wooden swing on the verandah. It's a small miracle I never started smoking, she thought to herself as the steam coiled up from her cup. There on the swing, in the shade of the porch, it was the first time in a while she'd really noticed the house from the outside. She'd nearly forgotten the dip of the wood, or the cut of the faux-Doric columns by the steps, or even how dark the varnish on the front door still was after all these years. All that sun and rain. Our little olive house, she was thinking, really it had used to be quite green—a rich royal green that would make you think of forests in the rain. Now the sun had all but bleached it dry, down to a pale olive straining to keep its tint against the weather. Oh, that light's gone out again too, she noticed, ashamed of instantly thinking how Evan oughta get it fixed sometime soon; same with the front door which still didn't quite shut all the way. But what can you expect from these old houses, really. They were made for another time entirely. It's a wonder they're all still standing, any of these on the block. This whole neighborhood even, right down to the property lines where Park runs into the highway and all the ghostly little houses drop off the cul-de-sac into the weeds. How many of them are even still full besides our own. I always did like that blue one down the way, with the metal sconces by the door. The little iron gate. But nobody's come out that door in years, have they; no, I haven't seen a soul that way in years. Always liked the little German villa-style house across the street too, with its sloping rooves and high steeple. If only they'd do something about that siding though, before it peels itself off on the lawn. Still, they were good people, that family; the Johnsons was it, or the Jamesons, I can't remember, haven't seen them in ages either. They were always throwing barbecues, bringing over plates of ribs for Mother cause they remembered back when Dad owned the smokehouse. Times were different back then, weren't they; things always happening. But now what is it. Just this, is all. Just this.

She started to check back on the mailbox again but something across the way had caught her eye. There was a dark shape across the intersection, in Miss Yvonne's old lot at the corner. At first it looked like the streetsign bending lower in the wind, but it was thicker than that—a pink shape billowing against the grass. It too was bent over, turned in profile, the shape of an old woman draped in faded wool, shuffling up the walk. Something in her step was purposeful, like she meant to be there, was in fact searching for something in particular; Eleni had seen that walk somewhere before. Now what's that old woman doing there, Eleni thought as she watched her amble closer to the house. Does she live there, across the way, in that busted old duplex, alone. Is she the one who tore the board down. Does she live in the gut of that ruin. Has she been living there all this time—.

The woman stopped like she'd heard Eleni's thoughts in her ear. She turned around completely to face her, a pink smudge across the way, palms open and outstretched at her knees, the wind making a thick slap of the wool. Eleni couldn't see her eyes but she knew that they were on her. That they held her there. There was nobody else on the block—not a single soul walking or driving or sitting on their porch. And the whole neighborhood was quiet but for the barking of a pack of dogs somewhere unseen. It was worse than the call of the loon—not a lonely cry but something more desperate, the hungry yapping of a whole host of creatures hollering at once. Eleni kept looking and the sun knelt down behind a thick cloud, a low weight of dirty vapor come off the lake to settle at this very crossroads. Eleni's forearms rattled with the old anxiety, sloshing her cold chai onto the porch. She gripped the mug tight in her hands. Tried to bring herself back to her body. But then a big wind swelled up and she hardly noticed it had ripped the mug out of her fingers until she heard it shatter on the floorboards at her feet. She looked at her hands, empty. At the shattered mug. The chai was seeping down through the splintered boards, and as it drained away she saw a familiar shape among the ceramic pieces. It was a little plastic locomotive—one of Jr.'s toys, the treasure he'd been looking for in the willow tree. Josiah'd brought it for them once, for their birthday. She picked it up, felt the weight of it in her hands. The blue wheels, the white smoke coming up out the spout. But how, Eleni thought, that's not—there's no—. She looked back to the vacant lot and the old woman slowly brought her hands back together, so that only her face was visible underneath the faded pink wool. She turned her back to Eleni and the vacant lot came awash with all kinds of bright light from inside the gutted house—lights that might have shot from gleaming chandeliers, a roaring hearth, torches by the entryway, floodlights from fixtures never mounted or else torn down years ago in the property's condemnation. Is it you, Eleni thought, not knowing what she meant by it. Is it really, really you—.

The cloud dropped suddenly right on top of the house. It seemed to crawl down straight out the sky, wrapping up the house in a mist so thick all the glaring lights were scrambled in its folds. The dogs kept on barking. Eleni clutched Jr.'s toy in her palm and turned around and ran straight through the house, where the basement door hung open on its hinges. She had locked it before, she knew. And she stepped forward but she couldn't step down, just stood frozen at the landing while the house creaked against the wind. From the basement came a heavy wave of moss, the smell of damp earth and cold stone. And it wouldn't let her pass.

From the shadows, Kitchen shot up the basement stairs out the dark, spilled herself between Eleni's legs. The cat bolted up the stairs and down the hallway into Evan's study, where finally she pressed her nose to the window, scanning the yard in wait for the rest of them. But all she saw outside was sky, a truck rattling through the crossroad, the sun coming down through a thin patch of cloud.

The men had come back from their lunches
heavy in their overalls   dusty gloves   hardhats slick
with pulling buckets of grey stone from the bowels of
the vacant duplex.   A low family
of sheetgrey stratus gathers to witness
the house's gutting.   One man directs the disposal truck
beeping in a fresh metal waste bin   while the old bin
light blue & draped in punctured tarp   clangs away
towards the mountains where some other house
keeps to itself.   A window left open
down the block spills out a Cher rendition into the street—
*Then I'm walkin' in Memphis   walkin' with my*
*feet ten feet off of Beale.*   The album cover overexposed & blue
on an armchair somewhere   Cher in her whiteblue slip with the snake
the apple—   It's a Man's World.   The clouds drink up the whole sky
&  the truck rumbles away with its clutch of
the ruined house—   *Walkin' in Memphis   but do I really*
*feel the way I feel*

## .VI.

Evan was the one to find her, asleep on her arms at the kitchen table, when they'd returned from the lake with the twins.

– El, you alright, Evan asked, shaking his sister awake.

– Is it done, Eleni cried.

– Wake up sleepyhead, it's just us, you must've had a bad dream.

Evan could tell the fear in his sister's face and so he drew his fingers through her bangs, sweeping the strands behind her ear. She is tired, he thought, but he knew there was something else. She's in one of her states again, he worried, knowing it would take her some time to come back to them.

– Oh, Evan, I was scared stiff. I was waiting on the laundry but I had no idea when you'd come. How late is it now, are the twins ok, did I—.

– Everything's fine, Ellie, Evan said, still smoothing out her hair. We had a lovely day at the park together, didn't we.

Effie and Jr. stepped forward together, their palms in each other's hands; Eleni had never seen them like that in all her years. Jr. had something in his hand she could tell he wanted to give her. He cut a look at Effie asking for permission to be the one to give it and something in her look back at him said of course so he stretched out his hand.

– We found it by the water, Jr. said. We thought you'd like it.

Eleni held out her own palm and accepted a smooth little stone of some mineral she couldn't place. It was heavier than she imagined from its size, and very dark, but a thin vein of rainbow streaked itself longways across the middle. She hadn't the first idea what to do with it or how to tell them thank you. She could see them in their thick overcoats trudging along the water scanning the rushes or playing their games and looking for something to bring back special just for her—a thought that dropped so heavy in her chest she couldn't tell did she want to cry or dance around the room. Instead she just smiled at them both. Evan chimed in to smooth his sister's silence for the twins, knowing she wouldn't know what to say.

– Found it while we were feeding the ducks by the lake, isn't that right Jr.

– Fat ducks, Jr. said, which got a rise out of Effie too.

– Got a good shot of em both by the banks, Josiah said, stepping forward with a Polaroid in his hand.

Eleni had hardly noticed him leaning there behind the others in the kitchen threshold and suddenly she felt guilty about that. Draped in the long green parka her dad used to wear, the camera slung across his chest, Josiah's eyes took on a warm gleam she hadn't noticed before and she was grateful that those eyes had seen her brother. She took the photo from his fingers.

There were her babies right there, stood side by side, looking into Evan's camera. Behind them she could make out the twisted trees at the lip of the lake, the sun softened by cloud. Effie was doing that little smile she had, with her mouth half opened, tiny teeth peeking through, her jacket zipped up to her chin. Beside her Jr. was looking wide-eyed, his head cocked towards his sister, the thin line of his lips caught somewhere between wanting to tell a secret and waiting for you to guess what it was.

But something's not right there. Something about it isn't them, Eleni thought, it's not them at all. Right there, in Jr.'s look—that same secretive look you always carried around, Mother, like the rest of us just weren't in on the joke. Something private, something you kept to yourself. But there it is, right there. That same look in my little boy. No, it's not right. I shouldn't have to see you like this, not in them too. Not in my children. Can't you just leave one thing for me without your fingerprints on it. Couldn't you just leave me this. They'll never even know you, Mother. They'll never even remember your face. You think they will but one day when I'm old and Thea's turned to dust they're going to forget all about your face and how kind you were to them, how much more careful and gentle you were with them than you ever were with us. One day, Mother, all the things you've done for them will disappear and they'll never even know it. That love, it'll all be shot one day. But I'm the one who'll have to see it. Their whole lives I'll be the one who's got to see you in them and remember you. I'm the only one. And I can't be the only one to remember you, Mother. I can't. Even Evan will forget one day. Even Thea will stop listening to you when you visit. The Daughters will stop checking in. Fanny won't answer my calls. And I'll be old and alone and I'll be the only one left to know you and I can't be the only one, Mother. It's not fair. It's not fair at all, making me see you again like this. No, I can't look at this photo any longer. I'll hide it away in a drawer somewhere; hide it away like I had to hide you; and I'll forget all about it, that's what. No, I can't look at them. I can't be the only one, Mother. I can't. I won't.

Jr. stepped forward, let go of Effie's hand. He had finally noticed the plastic locomotive in his mother's hand. She was gripping it tight against the rock.

– Ma, where'd you. . .the treasure. You found it.

Eleni met her son's eyes, her mother's eyes. She didn't offer him the toy.

– Where did you find it, Ma.

– Go to your room.

– Or did you take it. Did you take it out the tree.

– I said go to your room. I don't wanna hear a peep.

None of them spoke. A cloud passed over the windows. The twins stood quiet and the boys only watched Eleni stare down at the Polaroid. I know they'll be hurt, Eleni was thinking, all of them. I know they won't understand. But there's no way to give them this thing that I feel. There is no way to explain myself this time. But I simply can't bear it. I won't bear it. None of it is right. Not one thing about it's alright.

– You heard me, my babies, go to your room.

– But Ma.

– You heard me.

– El, what's wrong.

– Evan, don't.

– Ma.

– Go to your room.

–

–

–

–

– Did none of you hear me. Go to your room, please just leave me be. Please, please just go to your rooms, all of you. Go to your room, go to your room, go to your—.

The loon crashed into the kitchen window.

# CHORUS

Maybe now you see. Death it goes back a long way. And these Greeks they had plenty ideas about it. More'n just a stacking of years on top of years, the time can't nobody escape. Certainly none among us did. But Death it's also a place. Death it's also a house. That lonesome House in Hades, should the stories be believed. Maybe now you see it, at least a little.

The time passes on and then it doesn't. What's it matter to us anyhow. We just dip back into our corners. Some to the kitchen tile. Others to the sockets in the fixtures in the hall. We are there with the cat in the shadows, the sun. We measure the slamming of doors, visit the little woodfolk in the cuckoo clock's heart. And sometimes when the children gather round their books we gather round em too. Listen to the boy read out his stories—tales about heroes, monsters, gods, men, the shimmering mountains, the wine-dark sea, that lonesome House in Hades again, and the men come down to death together, alone, to drink from the pools of remember, the pools of forget. It's a goddess down there in the waters of death keeping record—the Muses' mother, Memory. And all the men across the ages keeping the stories alive, bound as they are on account of only living the one lifetime, they got to call on that goddess every time. Why, even you had to call upon us for this one. Anyhow a story's just a story. And most among us made our piece with that.

Still, some among us can't help but to wander. Only it's a couple places we no longer tread. Before, it was just us in between these walls. We got to know these wooden beams, these electric lights. We hummed together. Only now it's another one in here with us, the vibrations are changed. And we mean that very clear—the house is humming a different kind of way. She moves through the same walls and leaves smudges of her memory behind her. See em caked on fuseboxes and water pipes like crusted paint, flaking off in white and blue. And it ain't malicious, she don't mean no harm. Only a house can only take so much. This pool's not quite so deep, if you will. But we can dip inside it, yes we can. And we can go to her past, right here. Reckon we might as well bring you with us.

See what happens come time we make it back.

# KAIROS

The bells are ringing out across the village.

Sunday morning on the island of Lesbos, 1940, and all the streets are empty. Down in the harbor, the fishing boats creak against the wind, all of them painted white and blue, sloshing against their little wooden docks. The sails are all withdrawn, heavy spirals of frayed rope draped across the decks. A lone dinghy drifting off towards a row of buoys, weighed down with empty jugs, chipped oars and netting—the name EIPHNH streaked in blue across its hull. The gulls too are at rest, wings folded on the cobbles, watching the light come in across the water. The sea coughs up its weeds onto the rocks.

The village huddles itself tight against the slope of the hillside, as if it might one day slide into the sea. At the hilltop, the old castle crouches behind grey stone, sharp pines. The houses fray out from its perimeter, stone walls and clay shingles roped together with telephone wire. The houses, even the large ones, are old. They gather there like living things, tired from having strung themselves up out of the earth long ago, having collected their own walls out of brick, stone, plaster, assembling themselves from those same hillsides where they then crawled to settle back into the earth. Brick enclosures sit crumbling behind rusted fences, their wooden gates sunbleached and splintered. Windowboxes perch beneath missing pieces of glass, and the walkways are strewn with loose shingles. In the years to come, wild vines will push their way up from underneath some of the houses, and they will sit open and empty of people. Families will move, die out, forget, leave behind entire lots of cinderblock collapsed under the weight of some crawling root. In the years to come, construction projects will begin and then discontinue, unfunded. Concrete hollows never filled in, rooms never caked in human life. The buildings are all waiting, in their own ways, to be forgotten.

But everywhere is the heavy fragrance of flowers. Rosebushes crowd the telephone poles, and thick hedges of scrub peel apart the hills. Alyssum and wisteria choke the shaded patios in clouds of yellow and purple, and offroad, the anise sprout their thin stalks high up out the dust, spreading their white crowns wide. In the fields, donkeys and cats steal their shade from the squat olive trees, whose roots have been painted white to fend off the insects. In fifty years' time, these cobblestone alleys will buzz with Yamaha motorbikes, Kawasaki scooters, Suzuki vanettes. Merchants' sons buzzing between the remaining houses with figs bushels, loaves of bread, anything to net them some coins to bring home.

\*

In the center of the village, the bells keep ringing. Agia Barbara draws itself up, massive wooden doors open onto the marble columns, the courtyard. The elderly come dressed in black, the women in frocks and headscarves, the men's shirtsleeves rolled down. All of the windows are open but still the church is dark, cluttered inside with candlesmoke, wooden stands and gold basins. Marble arches rise high and turquoise above the frescoed walls, the saints all come together in wood and oil with their gold flecked halos and fetishes. A woman drops a coin into the dish, shuffles over to the side altar of Agia Barbara, where a full-sized effigy of the saint sits enthroned between golden pillars. The woman pulls from her pocket a small *tamata*—a thin piece of tin embossed with the image of a heart—and ties it with ribbon around a pedestal beside the icon. In a glass bell jar atop the pedestal, Agia Barbara's finger is enshrined, wrapped in cloth beneath another smaller golden dome. The woman crosses herself quietly in prayer and moves to kiss the icon, the jar. She rejoins the congregation.

Outside, soldiers rattle by in their motorized vans, hollering something.

\*

Afternoon, the sun high and hot. First meal of the day, after the body and the blood. Down by the harbor, the tavernas unfurl their tablecloths. The soldiers are hungry. German words, Italian words, salt and seagulls in the air. Somewhere there are children kicking a ball beside a fence. The same way that somewhere an olive drops into the harvest netting even though nobody is watching. In the hills, people move like shadows detaching from the trees. The villagers call them gypsies and sneer if they come too close. One of these women holds out her hand. There will come a time when somebody will have a little something to spare.

\*

There is a road off the main square leading away from the harbor up into the hills. The school is there, and a network of alleys strings together a small huddle of buildings. One of these is a blue house with a stone enclosure. Or maybe the house is white, and the blue is an illusion made by the weather, puffing up its ocean bruise in the sunshine. The trim on the windows, too, is a splintered blue. The curtains are some mesh color which, with enough exposure to the sun, will eventually bleach blue also.

A single lemon tree keeps the garden shaded, and an old man sits there in his wooden chair, smoking. Two other men walking down the street pass the gate to the enclosure and one of them calls out *Yiassou Evangelis* but Evangelis doesn't answer, he just keeps smoking. Inside the house, two young girls in the corner of

a room. They are each of them wearing the same simple dress, buttoned down to their shinbones. Dusty shoes, brown socks. Slender faces and brown curls. One of them is holding a bird, wrapped up in cloth. Moments before, it had flown against the window. When they went outside to pick it up it was breathing very fast and its eye was moving all over. The younger girl says nothing, watches her older sister try to feed it water from a spoon. After a few minutes, the bird stops breathing so fast. The older sister stands up, walks to the back of the house.

Evi where are you going, says the younger sister.

Get another spoon Sophia, says the older sister.

They are going to dig it a grave behind the house.

\*

Early evening, and the heat is settling back down into the dirt. At the end of the street, the phonelines make a black triangle against the blue sky, connecting both sides of the bend. At this small intersection, many of the old men might have claimed to see a saint walking around at dusk. Sometimes she is an angel disguised as a man, sometimes she is Agia Barbara herself, clutching thunder between her four good fingers. Sometimes she comes because of fasting in the heat, and sometimes she comes because of ouzo over ice. Still sometimes it might be said that she comes because the men only want for her to come. Right now, there is no drink on the card table. No saint wandering the roads. But there is a bright moon in the blue sky, watching the intersection from the space between the telephone wires.

With the men all gone together the women steal a moment to draw the curtains and read each other's coffee mud. A visitor, a change in weather, a small piece of bad news. The dog you know it's never a good sign. The snake it's ok. The bird it depends. Don't wash your hair after receiving a compliment. Don't wash your hands after giving one. Keep your shoes outside for the next three days. You going to lose some money if you don't.

\*

Far to the north, at the monastery at Mantamados, the monks are sweeping the courtyard. There are only a few pilgrims left inside the church, come to offer prayers to the Taxiarchis. A mother crosses herself and approaches the altar with a fresh pair of leather slippers in her hands. She kneels before the enormous icon encased in glass, kisses the ground, places the slippers beside a row of three other pairs, each newly made—the leather tight, stained dark brown; the nails driven in deep; the soles thick. Behind the glass, the impressive head of the Archangel Michael. Against the embossed silver of his armor, his wings, the jewels encrusted into his crown, his face is rust colored, severe. Behind the praying mother a father ushers his son forward, a firm hand between his shoulders. *It's a living Saint*, he is telling his son. *A body for Archangel Michalis, the commander, the warrior of God. You mother she's giving him fresh slippers because he walks around sometimes. And his shoes he wears them out. You can ask the monks to show you, they never throw out the old pairs. It's a holy thing she does.*

The son is watching his mother at the altar and listening to his father's story—how long ago a squadron of pirates landed on the beach and came to loot the monastery; how they cut the throats and spilled the blood of every monk they could find; how only one monk, a young novice, managed to escape up to the rafters; how he prayed to God for protection of His holy house; and how, at that moment, the Archangel Michael himself appeared above the sands and raised his golden sword against the sky and all the pirates dropped their loot and fled back to the ship, never to return. *The blood of those monks*, the father is telling his son, *it seeped into the sand and stained the courtyard. And that monk who survived to witness God's vision went down and collected the blood-soaked sand and made of it a kind of clay, and from this mixture he crafted the icon of the Archangel. Made for him a body here on earth, for him to walk around inside. He will protect us*, the father promises his son, *even from this.*

\*

At the westernmost point of the island, just north of Eresos, the sun is pouring its last light on the Petrified Forest. The earth there is rolled out in rich clay colored soil. Hardly any scrub crawls across those plains. But the trees, now stone-hardened, draw themselves up in columns older than the pillars of the most ancient temples. They might have taught the ancients a thing or two of veneration. Some lay sprawled along the shoreline, their exteriors bleached white, their rings pulsing pink and blue and yellow with the minerals they have become. Others still clutch the soil deep, reaching skyward in fists of deep amber, charcoal tinted. Three thousand years ago, the gods walked there in animal shapes. Forty years from now, the land will become a protected national monument. In this moment, it is still collecting light.

\*

Sun on it's way down and looking like thunder. Back in the village, all the shutters opening back up to let the heat out the houses. A woman in her little courtyard beating out the dust from her one good rug. She is old, and either doesn't see or pretends not to see a little girl patter down the alley by herself. Just *fwoo fwoo fwoo* the dust clouds coming out the rug.

Evi has it closed tight in her fist, the copper coin she found out behind the house one day. And she makes herself a little breeze across the cobblestones, the brick, the dusty roads. It's a straight shot to the Pappas house, then a left around the corner by the old Birakis place on the corner, now all but sliding into the grasses. From there it's just a matter of hiding in the scrub by the archway until the main road is empty—no soldiers in their shaky vans or friends of her uncle's. No men who might see a girl alone in the streets at night and think to make it their business. The streetlight hadn't come on yet, so she scurried across the broad back of the main road without making so much as a shadow.

Across the street there it was—the old Grammatis house. Some cousin on her mother's side according to Theo Evangelis. Some cousin, some mother she would only hear about. Paraskevi was her name, that long-dead cousin of her long-dead mother. And she lived in that house before. She was a holy woman, they said. She saw a vision of her namesake in the well, they said. Said she spoke to Agia Paraskevi herself, asked her for gifts of healing. Theo Evangelis knew her, but that was long ago. *That's where you name come from*, he told her once. *You Mama she gave you that name. You got to keep it good.*

The house is a tiny church now, ever since the family died. One single room with a window, a roof. She is very careful when she opens the door not to make any noise. Inside, the walls are yellow with smoke. She finds the matchbook by the basin of sand and lights the big candle. Drops her coin in the bowl. There is the usual altar, the usual icons. The Mother, the Child, the Archangels both. None of it gold. But in the center there she is—the icon of Agia Paraskevi herself. Story goes her cousin Paraskevi Grammatis saw a vision from the dry well, told the men to go down and bring back what they found there. And it was this icon they returned with. A small block of wood, weather-eaten and scuffed. The oil chipped off in huge fragments. Occasional specks of gold around the borders, a swath of faded maroon in one corner. There is a patch of blue paint so faint it threatens to shatter eggshell-like at the touch. The only part of the saint's body still there to see—the eyes. They come out of the wood their own golden brown, unblinking. Untouched by the seasons. This is how they knew she was true. Healer of the blind, restorer of sight, physician of light Agia Paraskevi. She who could not be burned by the tar and oil. She who was strung above the fires by her hair and was not licked. Tender of wounds, this ancient witch of God. She was eventually beheaded and so in some depictions carries her eyes on a silver tray in her palm. But always they are unmistakable. In the tiny room, clusters of silver tamata embossed with open eyes are fixed to every surface. The entire room flickering, watching, still.

Evi kisses the icon, the eyes. *Remember us*, that's all she asks. She snuffs the candle, closes the door, leaves the well alone. The streetlight comes on while she's hiding beside it, looking for men on the main road. It splashes her shadow around her, a star of little shadow girls stretched out across the dust. She runs home as fast as she can.

\*

Full moon, deep dark. Back at the blue house, the sisters are quiet on their cot in the shed. A family of cats has crept in, watching them from a pile of hay in the corner. Evangelis is in the kitchen presenting food to the soldiers and so has not noticed Evi's departure or return. But Sophia is quiet in that way that has a target attached.

I don't believe you, Sophia said when Evi told her.

But it was her, Evi said back, I felt her there. She heard me. She turned on the light behind me.

You could have—Sophia started to say, but couldn't finish the sentence. Evi had only looked at her.

From the house they can hear the soldiers throw their words around like stones. Evangelis will remain in the house until all the food is eaten, the dishes cleaned, the soldiers given their blankets and whisky. Eventually, the only thing to hear will be Evangelis running the faucet, the house settling into itself. Until then, they lay together on the cot looking up at the chord dangling down from the ceiling, its lightbulb dead now all summer. Outside, the night noises were getting bigger. Creak of bugs in the trees, bushes swooshing against the shed. Far away, overhead, a metal beast cuts across the night sky with its propellers, splitting the air into sheets of sound.

It's us, Evi says to her sister in the dark.

In the next ten years, Evangelis will arrange a marriage for one of them to an American businessman; he will do this by sending photos of the girls across the sea in the breast pocket of a younger cousin's jacket, the instructions—pick one; and the American man, Cecil Warren, will choose the photo on the right, of Evi, but he will agree to let the other one come too; the girls will pack all their belongings into a single crate, board a ship to New York, promise to write; Cecil will be there to meet them, and after the marriage is finalized he will drive them back down to his home in the mountains of East Tennessee; Evangelis will die and his grave will go unmarked; when the war is over the soldiers will leave the house to its eventual collapse. But at this moment, none of that is known. At this moment, it is simply two sisters on a cot in the shed beside their uncle's home, listening to the night.

After some time, the dead lightbulb begins to glow on its own. Warm orange eye in the dark shed. I see you, says the light. I will remember, says the electric hum. It's you. Look, Evi says to her sister, I told you. But Sophia has already fallen asleep.

MNEMÓSYNON

Another month & the weather is back.    This weather
this time    graying out the space between buildingspeopletrees.
Idle trucks winking down the alleys    the one good bulb in the mist &
everywhere the scrape of busted metal clanging the pavement
metal electric beeping    metal hollows    a chorus of metal
& exhaust.    They are still pulling out the innards
of the gutted house—    workers with their iron rods    scraping
wires lights insulation bricks plaster drywall screws
mist & light stealing through the exposed ceiling    a branch or two &
in the street another rectangular metal belly    waiting to be filled.
The men collect the bones the sinew the joints
the heart of the dead house.    Years ago that family
hung potted ferns by the windowsill    lit candles in the foyer
measured their children against the blue wallpaper.

.I.

—It's a crying shame, Fanoula, that's what it is.

Eleni was crouched in the kitchen, pulling mixing bowls out from under the counter, the telephone receiver pinched between her cheek and shoulder. It was early still, just after 8 o'clock, but she couldn't sleep anyhow. Evan tried to keep the twins quiet while getting them dressed for school earlier, but they never could hold still around him, he made them laugh too easy. Eleni had just laid there and listened to the whole thing, pretending she might drift back off at some point. Really she just watched the light getting brighter and listened to their boots leave the house, each to their separate buses. But it didn't matter. Besides, she had meant to wake up early and give that priest another call. It was Good Friday, April 14th, and she knew he'd be awake before the morning service. After three rings unanswered she decided to call up her cousin.

—I mean it's pitiful, Fanoula, it's really just pitiful. The man's a priest for crying out loud, the very least he could do is call me back. Or pick up the phone when I call. Am I not still part of the church, just cause we haven't been in a while. They all know about Thea, about her hip. God knows the Daughters' Association keeps calling and calling. Vultures, those women. I swear, sometimes I think they're just waiting around for Thea to kick it so they can be the first to spread it around. You should have heard Theodora the other day, asking me was Thea planning on renewing her Daughters membership any time soon. I said to her you know what Theodora, I don't think she does plan on renewing that membership after all so I guess this is one less number you got to bother calling. I wish to God I coulda seen her face, Fanoula, really I do. I bet her jaw just about hit hell.

Fanny couldn't help but laugh across the line.

—Come on now, *agapi'm*, don't talk like that.

—You know it's true! These women. But that Theodora especially. She's the mouth of the south, that one. I'm sure they're all the same down there in Easton as they are up in Bristol.

—Well, maybe. But you shouldn't talk like that. Especially now. It is Holy Week, after all. Good Friday, no less.

—Don't remind me.

—You ever think maybe that's how come the Patera isn't calling you back. I mean it's the busiest time of year for the priests, during Lent. Services sometimes three four times a week you know. Why, I don't know how father Gabriel does it most days, what with his foot and all. You know he's got that limp.

—Well, thank you for the Sunday school lesson *Presbytera mou*, are you sticking around for coffee hour.

—Eleni Warren, you watch that tongue! It's a sin, talking like that.

—I know.

—I'm not saying it's right, all I'm saying is cut the man a piece a slack.

—I know. It's just—you know, he said he was gonna come bless the house after that incident with the loon. Said he'd call me back later in the week, and do you think he did. Course not. Now, is it too much to ask for the priest to keep his appointments. It's bad luck, Fanoula, having a bird break its neck on your window like that. Bad omens, you know that. Haven't been able to sleep a wink, and God knows what's going on in my dreams. I just think it's the least he could do, to come put some peace of mind back into this house. You know he was supposed to be coming out here once a month to give Thea some communion. Once a month, Fanoula, that's it. He can't drive a couple hours to feed a sick lady the sacraments she deserves, well, I don't know what kinda priest he thinks he is.

—Nitsa, I love you, but I don't know what to tell you.

—Well.

—I don't suppose y'all are making it to the service tonight.

—No, I don't suppose we will.

—Well, that's alright. It's a nice service. Sad. But I always did like it, especially the midnight service tomorrow. That one's always nice too, walking around the church like that at night. All those candles going. The boys carrying the *epitaphion*. And the hymns!

—I know.

—Those are some of my favorite hymns they ever sing, all year. So pretty, so full. You ever wonder how come the sad ones are always the prettiest to hear. How come they feel so good to sing along to.

—I don't know, Fanoula. I don't really remember em all too well.

—Hmm.

—You know—.

—What is it.

—It's just—.

—Awh baby, don't cry now. Come on, what's a matter.

—It's just, you know, she woulda been ninety years old this year.

—I know it, *koukla*.

—Her birthday woulda been this Sunday. And they're supposed to be doing a *mnemosynon* for her at the church in September, cause then it'll be two years.

—Well, that's always a nice thing, the memorial service. You should get Thea Sophia to help you with the *koliva*.

—I can't do it, Fanny.

—You got to, Eleni.

—I can't do it.

—Eleni you got to listen to me one minute ok. That's an important thing to do, for your mother's soul. Do you even know how important it is. *Mnemosynon* means *memory*, Eleni. And it's up to you and Evan and Thea Sophia and the twins to keep Thea Evi alive in your memory. It's up to you and nobody else to pray for her every day. Ask the angels, ask the *Panagia*, ask the Lord to remember your mother in His kingdom for all the good things her hands have done Eleni cause once we go I'm telling you that's all we got left is the prayers of folks we leave behind. Your mother needs you to pray for her and she's gonna need you to suck it up and make that *koliva* for her eternal soul, you hear me.

—I know it's important, Fanoula, you don't need to tell me about it. But I just don't know how I'm going to—oh you know I want to go to the service tomorrow too, I really do, I know she'd want me to go but Fanny I just can't I mean I just can't even think about it I mean how am I supposed to show my face there now, how am I supposed to go sit in that church tonight or tomorrow night or Sunday especially knowing that her birthday falls on Easter this year and she's not—oh it's sick Fanny that's what it is it's sick and it's not fair cause it's supposed to be Easter and it's supposed to be her birthday and she won't even be here for it Fanny I'm just sick to my stomach I mean really just sick to my stomach and I don't, I just don't—oh, Fanoula, I just don't know how I'm going to do that day.

—Alright baby alright, calm down. Just breathe a little ok. You are gonna do just fine this year, you hear me. I'm sorry to get stern with you. Come on now. Here's what you're gonna do. You're gonna straighten up and whip up this coconut cake for Thea Evi and that's a good thing you're doing. We'll worry about the *mne-*

*mosynon* in September alright. Now you got to stop crying now, you hear me, cause you need to focus. Can't be making a bad cake, alright. You got to make it good for your mother.

—I know—.

—She always did like that coconut cake.

—I know—.

—So you got to just keep your eyes dry and focus on making it, you hear me. *Eleni mou*, do you hear me.

—I hear you, Fanoula. I'm sorry, I—I'm sorry I get like this.

—Quit saying you're sorry, Nitsa. How many times I need to tell you, it's alright. But you just got to work through it. That's all you got to do.

—I know, you're right. Thank you. I'm so sorry, calling you so early in a mess like this. But thank you.

—It's alright, like I said. You're gonna be just fine. Anyway I got to let you go, Nitsa. It's a big weekend at the mall and I'm trying to make those numbers.

—Alright. I love you. Try and not work too hard.

—We'll see.

—Oh wait.

—What is it.

—Remind me again about that cake. It's vanilla *and* almond extract, right.

—Well, I suppose you don't need em both. But I do like the almond, gives it a certain, I don't know. Just use what you got, Nitsa. It'll be fine.

—Dagummit. I don't have vanilla or almond. Where all my stuff's gone I just don't know.

—Well.

—I'll just have Evan pick some up for me today from the Foodland. Maybe Josiah can—.

—Do what now.

—Nobody. I mean, nothing. Thanks Fanoula. Love you, take care.

—Love you too, Nitsa. Now don't forget to whip those eggs up good. Really beat the fire out of em.

—Alright, bye-bye.

—Bye-bye.

Eleni hung the receiver back on its hook, stood looking at the spread of ingredients and kitchenware laid out on the table in front of her. Mixing bowls, one large for the batter, one small for the eggs. Three sticks of butter, warming up to room temp. Glass measuring cup, the red gauges almost all but worn off from too much washing. Baking powder, baking soda, that big bag of flour. The salt grinder, *thalassino alati*. Cream cheese. Coconut flakes. Her mother's wooden spoon, snapped into a crescent moon shape against Evan's backside when they were little. Her mother. She picked up the wooden spoon, set it back down. Outside there was a rumpled mist making its way down off the mountains. She looked down the street as a man in an orange vest crossed the intersection from the vacant lot, probably headed to the drug store for a coffee. Least it's not that loon, she thought, screaming with those red eyes. But still—still it shouldnt've gone and killed itself against the house. It's bad omens, that's what. She pinched her fingers together and quickly did her cross across her chest. But that didn't change anything, did it. No, that didn't change a thing at all.

Hold on now, this is supposed to be a good thing I'm doing. Mother wouldn't get all bent outta shape on account a some bird. She'd just whip up the cake one two three just like that and sit down with some coffee on the porch. That's what she'd do. Hell with the bird. Hell with that house too. They can tear the whole thing down for all I care. See if I mind. Anyway it's the batter first. Or is it the eggs. Got to get ahold of Evan about the extract. Or maybe it doesn't matter. Hold on now, I know what let's do—. We'll have a little music. Now where'd I put those speakers, up front I think. They must be up there somewhere.

When she stepped into the foyer she caught the light coming through the window curtains making a lake on the bedsheets, rumpled and bunched together. Had she gotten up before Evan he would have thought to make the bed. His boots stood together beside the nightstand, in their own place. And there was his hardback, closed and framed right in the middle of the wood. But it was the cabinet she needed, at least that's where she remembered seeing it last. At the back of the room, by the couches wrapped in plastic and the wall of family portraits, the big black laquered cabinet. The top half was fit with glass, little golden knobs on the doors, where she kept all her mother's good china. She tried not to look at it too long. The doors on the bottom half were wooden, carved into with the shape of flowers. And there it was, right where she left it—that big grey boombox tucked in the back, all her old tapes. She had plenty left over from the nineties, cassettes and CD reissues both. Joni Mitchell, Dolly Parton, Sonny & Cher, even those miserable old Greek folk singers her mother used to play while fixing dinner.

She remembered cracking open the jewel case to *Blue* one day down in Easton with Fanny and all her girlfriends from high school. Fanny was a clean ten years older than her, and Eleni had never been with the big girls before. It was the first time she'd ever heard the words booze and ass, let alone coming so pretty from a song. The girls had stolen a single cigarette from Uncle George's pack, took turns blowing smoke out Fanny's bedroom window, all pretending to be Joni putting on her silver, waiting for her mean old daddy down at the Mermaid Café. *It sure is hard to leave you, but it's really not my home.* Had she been in the kitchen she would've called Fanny back up right then and there, just to ask her did she remember that day. But Fanny's got better things to do than get back to all that. And I got a cake to bake. She popped her copy of *Heartbreak Express* into the boombox, carried a handful of tapes with her back to the kitchen. *I'm gonna roll on down the line. I'm gonna go so far I'm gonna get it off my mind.*

It was the music that woke up Thea.

The wind she didn't mind. And the construction workers outside she could tune out. What was the breaking of wood to her, anyway, the clamor of metal. But that whining saxophone, that *thumpa thumpa thumpa* of the standup bass. Too early for all that. She pulled aside the covers and swung her feet to the floor and sure enough it was that bright purple pain in her hip. A breeze coming through the window poofed up her pink nightgown but still the pain was too hot to cool. *Och, Panayia'm*—she rolled it in the back of her throat like a small curse, one of the virgin mother's many handles—*Ever-Blessed, All-Holy*. How many names does she need. *Theotokos*, Mother of God in the scripture, *Agni Parthene Despina* in the songs. Must be better up there, is it nice. What you think about it, Evi, is it nice. Sophia turned her great head to the rug at the foot of the bed. The treadmarks were fresh again this morning. What would you know, Sophia thought, if it's nice up there. You never lay down, Evi. You never went. You just keep hanging around here, what would you know. She reached over to the end-table by the bed—dark-stained wood, brass knobs on the drawers, all her own icons arranged. First thing she did was crack open her *thimiato*—that once-golden censor, egg shaped, topped with a smokestained cross. It had become difficult to open over the years, caked through with soot and dried resin. It had burnt through generations of incense, and just to crack it open would release that warm smell. But still she would light it anyway. You know, Sophia was thinking as she unwrapped the little charcoal medals from their brown paper, today it's a holy day. The charcoal clung to her fingers and she brushed the stray flecks off onto her nightgown, smearing the pink. They supposed to put the Lord in the tomb tonight, she thought, setting a match to the charcoal. From a plastic bag she fingered two small shards of incense to place on the charcoal. A pink resin, coated in white, they looked like miniature Turkish delights. Sophia cupped her palm around the censor and puffed to encourage the flame and sure enough the incense came spilling up a thick cloud into the room. They gonna carry him around the church and then they gonna put him in the ground, Evi. She strained to push herself fully up off the bed and clutched the censor tight in her fingers. They gonna put him in the ground, and he gonna come back because that's what he can do. You think you like the Lord, Evi. You think you can just come back. She made the sign of the cross with the censor, first over the bed, then the end-table, then the door to the attic turret. It was hanging open on its hinges, thin sheets of light coming down the stairwell from the windows at the top of the house. If you gonna stay up there, Evi, stay put. You think you can hang around forever. In the back of her throat Sophia began to hum the antiphons. But downstairs it's that hillbilly trash, she thought, that *Americaniko garbish*. You hear that Evi, that's you daughter down there. Making all that noise on a day like this. Sophia reached for the attic doorknob. A pipe groaned in the walls. She pulled the door shut. You heard me.

Eleni was in the middle of mixing the batter, the electric beater whirring on high against the bowl. She had changed the tapes over from Dolly to *Dinner in Greece*. She couldn't hear it too clear through the beater, but still she picked up the rhythms, did the dance steps in place beside the table. Evan had taught her this one when they were kids, right here around this very table. It was an island dance, an *ikariotiko*, and Eleni loved the steps because they were simple and fluid, how she imagined the waves of the sea, a little bit forward a little bit back. Evan always used to dance it at the festivals growing up. Had a certain grace none of the other girls could match, let alone the boys. She saw him now for a moment back then, his curls wet and springy, sweat coming down through his white oxford, unbuttoned. Evan floated right through that dance, the drone of the lyra's strings and that steady strum like water under the balls of his feet.

There, she thought, that oughta do it.

She turned off the electric beater and the music came in big and full. She licked one of the whisks and before she could think too hard about it she started to dance around the kitchen. Her feet swept across the tile, trying to match that gentle bob in Evan's step. How long had it been, she couldn't even say. And it did feel nice, didn't it. It did feel good.

She smelled the smoke before she saw her. Thea was standing at the kitchen threshold, charcoal smeared across her pink nightgown, incense pluming out from the censor in her fingers. Eleni nearly tripped over her own two feet rushing to turn the volume down.

—*Kalimera Thea*, she said.

Thea didn't look at her. She was fixed on the mess at the table, bowls and eggshells dripping onto the wood.

—How do you feel, Eleni said.

Thea shuffled over to the window, made a cross with her censor in front of the glass. The track on the tape changed. Some gentle glittering on the bouzouki.

—I thought I'd make us a coconut cake, Eleni said. You know, cause—well. It's Ma's birthday coming up and all. You know she always did like a nice coconut cake.

Thea turned around but still wouldn't catch Eleni's eye. She was looking at the boombox.

—I'm sorry if I woke you up, Thea. I should have—I know it's early. I just thought I'd—.

—You know what day it's today, Thea said.

—I—.

—You know what day it's today.

—Of course, Thea. It's Good Friday.

—Today it's a holy day.

—I know.

—They putting the Lord in the tomb today.

—I know.

—Do you know, Thea said, looking Eleni in the eye. Today it's a day of mourning. They putting the Lord in the ground. Nobody thinking will he come back. Nobody believing the prophets. And certainly nobody making cakes, dancing around. Everybody in mourning. You understand.

—Of course, Thea. I just thought we'd have us a little—.

—You not supposed to be playing music today neither.

—I'm sorry, Thea. I'll turn it off.

They both stood there, not moving. Watching each other.

—Supposed to be fasting, too, Thea said. Cake it's no good. Milk, eggs. What, you think this some kind celebration.

—Thea, come on now, I said I'm sorry. I told you, it's for Ma.

—You mother gonna eat it then, this cake. She gonna come up out the ground like the Lord on Easter Sunday just to eat this cake.

—Thea—.

—You mother she was too easy on you, Eleni. Didn't teach you right. It's not you mother's house anymore. You got to quit doing these things. Encouraging it. She got to lay down, you know. Nobody coming back but the Lord. You want to do something for you mother, pray He remembers her. Go to church. Light a candle. That's it. When it's time, we all got to lay down. Now clean up this kitchen. You wanna bake something, make the sweetbread for Sunday. Or maybe you don't remember.

Eleni was looking at the kitchen tiles like she might crack one under the pressure. She bit her lip, didn't say anything.

—What time Evangelis through with work, Thea asked. You brother, he gonna take me to the service tonight. We not gonna miss it again this year.

Thea turned her back and started shuffling towards the foyer, so she could cense the rest of the house; through the walls, Eleni could still hear the antiphons creaking out of her chest. From the boombox, that same swell of the lyra's strings. But the waters under her feet had receded.

Top of the house the metal weathervane creaking
west & south & west on the turret squeaking
street  street  street  snow  street  dew  street
still street underneath the warping beams.     The wind it
pulls the clouds down like brillo scrubs.
It's a tindrum pebble in a dish kind of rain coming.
That metal bird squeaking the concrete street   street
street down below.

## .II.

By noon Eleni had at least managed to gather up all the mixing bowls and utensils into the sink. All the ingredients still there on the kitchen table though. Vanilla, sugar, eggs. She'd started to clean herself an apple but she left that on the table too, only half-skinned. To hell with the stupid cake, she thought, running hot water from the tap. She was tonguing the backs of her teeth, jaw clenched tight. But her eyes were unfocused. Who does she think she is, Eleni thought; but also—what was I thinking. The anger and embarrassment both swam across her eyes in equal measure. So be it. She just looked out at the lawn. The workers were all sat on the curb in front of the gutted house, taking their lunches from brown bags. Noon already, she thought, the twins'll be home soon and I haven't hardly done a thing around this house. They'll want something to eat, I guess. I'll have to fix em something. She just kept looking out at the lawn.

The glass they'd gotten to replace the kitchen window was thicker than the old. Eleni couldn't place it exactly, but it was something to it made everything sharper, brighter, clean. She didn't like it. It called too much attention to itself. And the windows on the back door still dusty and smudged. The scum in the sink, the blackened cracks of the tiles, all this she started to notice ever since that new window. She cursed the loon again under her breath. Sometimes when she stood at the sink washing dishes she'd see it flash by all over again—the bird getting bigger and bigger until its full weight shocked the glass to pieces. Evan had to be the one to go outside and see was it still living or not, that day. It was a blood smear across the faded siding that took him at least a week to get out. Eleni didn't know what ever happened to the body and she didn't ask.

—Oh!

Kitchen had snuck across the tile between Eleni's legs, her tail making goosebumps on Eleni's skin.

—Christ, Eleni said, scared the fire outta me stupid cat. Don't tell me, you need something from me too.

Kitchen only craned her neck up, those glowing green eyes unblinking.

—Figured as much. Alright, come on now.

Evan kept Kitchen's food in a pantry opposite the basement door, her dish and a little bowl of water tucked discreetly in the corner. Eleni hoisted the heavy bag onto her hip, shook out the dry food in such a way that most of it ended up in the floor.

—There. Something extra, free of charge.

Kitchen nosed the pellets and twitched her ears, wouldn't take a bite until Eleni looked away.

—Oh fine, stubborn cat. Suit yourself. Got better things to do anyhow.

Eleni turned away from the pantry and nearly hit the basement door head-on, hanging open on its hinges. She hadn't even heard it swing out. She looked at the lock, one of those cylinder latches that takes a little work to open up. It had been closed before, hadn't it, she thought, or did I forget to latch it back when I—when I—when was the last time I even went down there. The light coming in through the kitchen window and the front door somehow only magnified the shadows in the basement stairwell. They were thick, like the damp cold coming up off the underground concrete. The April mist only thickening the chill earth smell further. What, Eleni half-whispered, what do you—.

Kitchen turned her head towards the stairwell, one paw frozen in midair, as Eleni took a step down. Then another. Before she knew it she was at the landing, looking down at the laundry machine. She hadn't used it lately, hadn't run a load in days. But still there was this low hum rattling through the metal, some dull noise behind the white exterior. The old wood sighed beneath her footsteps, but she kept descending, her hand on the rail. And there it was, that same old Whirlpool her mother had bought back in '84. She placed her hand on the machine, felt the hum, smelled the detergent. *Eleni-mou*, she heard a voice inside her ears, *throw it down you sheets. Tell you brother bring me his socks*. No, Eleni thought, be quiet. She turned to go back up the stairs but stopped, looking out into the rest of the basement. The shadows wrapped it all up in a vague outline of boxes, furniture, looming shapes in the thin light from upstairs, a little skyline of the past right there in front of her. She took a step into the dark, though something about the clutter made her feel she couldn't pass, couldn't go any further. Still there was that voice again, *Just wind it up baby'm, you know how to do it*. Out of the shadows, as if it had only just appeared, Eleni saw the tarnished horn coming up off the old victrola. *Go ahead, yem, wind it up*. It drew her step by step away from the washing machine, the concrete cold against her bare feet.

She used to keep the horn dusted you know, said the air inside the victrola. Used to keep the wood clean too, it said, and its lopsided leg agreed. She tried to save us too you know, from the damp, said the boxes of records on the floor, splotched with fresh condensation, threatening mildew. Over here! another voice from further back in the shadows, the sofa this time. You know she stitched up these arms herself real good—remember that Christmas and Evan took to the scissors. Remember my cushion. Eleni kept walking further into the clutter, not daring to touch a single thing even though the smell was all it took. She would have to get Evan down here to clean and that's all there was to it. How about sneaking home then, asked the oriental rug, rolled up and leaning into itself. Remember when you spilled all that beer. Your mother she scrubbed it and scrubbed it, got the whole stain out after you'd already gone up to bed. Thought you were sneaky but she knew. And she didn't say nothing neither, just took the stain out my fibers and went to bed herself. Once you made it home. It was alright after that. She could sleep. Oh but how about the time, said the green clock with the eagle talons, that time you said you wanted to hang me in your house so your ma she took me down. Took me down just for you and now here I am. Now where are your walls. Or what about me, the tiger mask said, how she took me off the wall cause your brother he was afraid. By now the whole basement began to speak, voice after voice, their visions rolling over each other in wisps, echoes, half-collected light.

    Remember when she [

               ] again with the Pine-sol

               ] that night when the power

    New Year's Eve 2001 remember that when she boiled the [

               ] when she made you that

               ] when she had all the

               ] and everyone was over

    It was a brand new iron [

               ] and nobody

               ] it was delicious

               ] she broke that spoon on his backside. She did

               ] and the Avon lady!

    All those boxes [

               ] and the little cows on the window

    Yvonne's boy what was his name the nice one with [

               ] the backyard, all those streamers

               ] used to picking figs out back

               ] those needles

    Glen doing the grass. She'd always offer him [

] mushrooms on those pillows. Remember the slug

] that roach in the microwave

Those jars from the village, a pair, one for sugar one for [

That story about the eagle [

She tried to teach them you know [

] the alphabet books

That trunk with all her postage peeling off it came from Mytiline [

] still those pink curtains

Remember at the christening she wore [

] remember at the wake

] always on your birthday

That watch she always took it with her, remember [

] her billfold

] her ticket over

] remember where she kept it. You shoulda taken it when you had the chance no telling where it is now.

] remember how

Remember when [

] check your pockets

] even though

The washing machine had been whirring on tumble dry the whole time and Eleni only just managed to turn and see it shaking at the other end of the basement. She was all the way back by the crawlspace, where bare earth broke against the foundations of the house. She pulled herself out of the clutter on cold concrete footsteps. All the while the Whirlpool was clanging around at the foot of the stairs. By the time she reached it, the green light had gone off and the rattling was still, the door unlatched on its own. All it took was to open the door, reach inside, see what was there. The chamber was empty as far as she could see, but she stuck her hand inside it anyway, feeling around the metal gut. There at the bottom, her fingers found a small coin—a dime wrapped up in tin foil. Her forearm twitched with that old anxiety—she recognized that coin. Another old tradition, every New Year's Day—the cutting of the *Vasilopita*, that sweet loaf, her mother surrounded by flour at the kitchen table, waking that next morning to cut the loaf into slices, one for the Lord, one for the Mother, one for the House, one for each member of the family, the living and dead, everyone secretly hoping to find this little coin baked inside their slice promising a whole year full of luck, and somehow her mother always used to win, didn't she, and every time Eleni would ask her *Mother how come you always get the coin* her mother she'd just shrug and do that motion with her lip, palms up, *Doxa to Theou, baby'm, my luck it's your luck too.*

Eleni clutched the coin so tight in her palm she thought she could feel the dime begin to bend, her footsteps back up out of the basement shaky, uncertain. At the top of the stair she closed the door behind her without having to look down into those shadows again. Evan'll just have to clean out that basement, she thought, locking the doorlatch behind her. There's just nothing else for it.

In the kitchen it was an unfamiliar rustling like an animal in the trash bins. Filled with some strange courage, maybe it was the dime or maybe something else, Eleni puffed her chest and stomped into the kitchen. We'll see about these animals, she thought. Not one more piece of trouble getting into this house. Just let em come and try it. When she turned the corner she screamed.

—Ma, where'd you go. We were waiting at the stop.

Jr. was crouched at the little cupboard under the counter, pulling out a box of Fruit-O's. Kitchen was curled in a puddle of sun by the back door, her usual spot in the late afternoon just before supper. She lifted her head, rested it back on her paws.

—What are you doing, baby.

—Getting cereal.

—No. No, I mean—what are you doing here. Where's your sister. You're supposed to be at school.

Jr. gave her one of his looks, lips together like he didn't wanna say it, the thing that he knew. Instead he just pulled the cereal out of the cupboard, tried to reach up to the higher shelves for a bowl. From the foyer, the cuckoo clock cooed one, two, three times, the springwork villagers all coming out of their houses into the town square, the woodsman knocking his axe against the stump three times, once for each hour after noon. Then the ritual was finished. The milkmaids, clutching their skirts, backed into the shed. The children froze mid-dance around the square, and they too retreated back behind their doors. Tick tock, three o'clock.

—Can you help me reach it, Ma. It's too high up.

Eleni dropped the dime onto the kitchen tile.

The street is choked with men    workers in vests
uniformed men with phones to their ears    men in heavy
boots & gloves latching metal chords to wooden planks
steel clamps securing the new scaffolding.    All through the air
that same electric hum    metal beeping    a heavy crane groaning
around the corner    pulverizing gravel in its tracks.    The crane's arm
reaching to collect some bundle of brick    interrupts the sunbeam
the shadow ticking across the neighboring houses like clock arms.

.III.

Upstairs, the twins were sat in the floor, a plate of half-eaten butter and jelly sandwiches pushed aside. Jr. was flipping through his storybook—*Gods, Monsters, Heroes & Men*. The spine was all but cracked in two from all the years. It'd been Evan and Ma's before, when they were little too. Jr. knew the pages backwards and forwards, could recognize every illustration, tell you every story, all the heroes' names, rattle off all the Gods' shapes and symbols. The heroes were fun sometimes, but his favorite chapter was the one on the Underworld, all the strange rivers and guardians, how it was out of sight but always there, how all the heroes and Gods had to deal with it eventually. He was absorbed now in one of his favorite drawings—Euridice getting sucked back down into Hades because Orpheus looked back to be sure she was there. Something about those shadows he liked. The way they looked like smudged flames, black flickers pulling her down underneath. He liked to tell that story to Effie sometimes, always blowing it up bigger and bigger. *And Or-fus*, he would say, *he had Erry-Dikky's hand right in his fingers, and his foot was even back up on the earth, in the grass! And they were right there, already home, thinking how they'd live in the trees and sing music to each other and have all the babies they wanted. But that's when Or-fus made his mistake. He was looking around all excited and he caught Erry-Dikky's face from the corner of his eye and then all the sudden fwoom! she was gone, just like that. You could hear the dogs barking to have her back, and from somewhere down deep, Or-fus could hear his voice—Hades, the God of death, all wrapped up in smoke saying I told you so, I told you you couldn't do it.* At this point Jr. would do one of his shrugs, whether Effie had stopped listening or not, and say something like, *so that was that. No more music for Or-fus.*

—Where do you think she was, Effie said.

—Huh.

—That whole time, what was she doing.

—She was s'posed to be following him up outta death.

—Not the storybook, I'm talking about Ma.

—Oh.

—Usually she's there.

—Yeah.

—What do you think she was doing.

—I don't know. What does she usually do.

—I don't know.

The windows creaked against a timid wind. Outside, the crane was still groaning with the weight of concrete and stone. Somewhere in the walls a pipe was making itself known. Jr. turned the page in his storybook and instantly Effie knew something was wrong.

—What is it.

—

—Jr., what is it.

—That's her.

—What do you mean that's her. That's who.

—Look. The ick-it. She's there.

Effie crawled beside her brother, took the book from his lap. He pointed to a sketch on the page, a charcoal shadow on the white paper. There was a woman there on the page, a drawing she didn't remember seeing before. The woman was draped in long robes, two dogs at her side, holding a torch in each hand. And the woman had three faces, one on each side of her head—a girl, a woman, an old lady. In little black letters under the photo it said: *HECATE, an offering at the crossroads.*

—Jr. are you sure.

—It's her, I know it.

—Did you see her.

—Yeah.

—That night you—.

—Yeah.

—Ok.

—She lives under the house.

—Ok.

—I mean it Effie. She took the treasure and she tried to drag me under there too and then she just.

—Just what, Jr.

—

—Jr.

—She's not going away.

Effie had seen this worry in her brother before. She was used to his quiet. But something about it now felt different. Not the usual. She half-started sentence after sentence in that silence but none of them would work out and so she just looked down at the book. What is it Jr., she wanted to ask. What are you keeping from me. And how come I'm afraid. How come I'm afraid of what you're afraid of but I don't even know what it is. You shouldn't keep it all, Jr. It's just me. It's us. It's us.

The rest of that day slid by in much the same mood. Kitchen occasionally flicked her tail in the sun, the twins up in their room in silence. Eleni she just sat at the kitchen table among the goopy eggshells and half-made batter. She was getting fruitflies already on account of the sugar. They dizzied themselves in front of her eyes and when they landed on her arms or cheekbones sometimes she made a move to swat them off but mostly she just sat there. Thea in her bedroom was laying out her clothes on the bed for the service later that night. The whole house, it seemed, was waiting for Evan to get home. The paint on the baseboards was only going to keep peeling, and that front door wasn't in any hurry to fix itself. The iron staircase was in want of a couple new screws, and the mailbox hadn't been opened in days. So much of the house was only a house when Evan touched it. And in it's own way, the house was worried too—worried every time he leaves that he just might not come back.

But Evan did come home that night, on schedule. He carried the day heavy on his face, though nobody was there to see it. *Hello*, he called into the house. No footsteps, no answer. Even Kitchen took her time to meet him at the banister. He watched her from the front door, jangling his keys in his pocket. He was dressed sharp as ever, but all the pieces were a bit off. His hair was a wild mess, and there was a run straight down the left shoulder of his sweater. Even his overcoat was creased, as if he'd tossed it aside and forgotten about it all day. He took a deep breath, steeling himself for the inevitable questions—how was work, how's Josiah, what time are you taking Thea to church. But he boxed his life up beneath an iron lid, dropped it deep in the pit of his chest. Now I have to see about the rest of them, he thought, as he slowly stepped into the kitchen.

—What's all this, he said to his sister, nodding towards the table.

—Oh, Evan, she said, a beat too late. You're back.

—Yeah, I'm back, now what's all this mess. Christ, Ellie, you're sitting in gnats. You know you can't leave this shit out like that. Eleni do you hear me.

—It was supposed to be for Mother, Eleni said.

—What was.

—You know how she always did like a coconut cake.

—A coconut cake.

—Mhm.

—And what made you decide to half-make a coconut cake.

—Do you really not remember, Evan, she said, turning in her seat. Do you really not know. Is it—is it so easy for you to just forget about it.

—Eleni will you spit it out. I don't know what hell you're talking about.

—Ma's birthday, Evan! Our mother! Tomorrow! Don't you get it.

—Eleni.

—No, don't Eleni me, Evan. She woulda been ninety years old tomorrow, you know that.

—Of course I do.

—Do you. Cause you just waltzed right into this kitchen and asked me with a straight face what the hell are you making a coconut cake for.

—Jesus, Eleni.

—Do not do that to me, Evan! Talk to me like I'm crazy. Shake your head every time she comes up. Wasn't she your mother too. Don't you miss her at all.

Had the two of them been listening more carefully they would have heard the twins' soft footpatter across the wood upstairs, returning to their secret spot at the top of the stairs. The doors themselves seemed to lean open, and the Frigidaire quieted its hum. The whole house leaned inwards to listen.

—Are we doing this now, Eleni. Do you really want to do this now. Of course I miss her. I miss her every single day.

—Is that right.

—Yes, yes I do. And don't you ever accuse me otherwise. You know what your problem is, Eleni—.

—I'll tell you what my problem is, Evan. It's this whole damn house! It's the busted door, that awful window, all Ma's shit just tucked away with nobody to give it to. And don't even get me started on that basement. I been after you for ages to help me go through all that shit, and do you think you have. No. You been too busy—

—*I* been too busy hauling my ass out to Johnson city on the goddamn Rover bus five days a week to make enough money to feed *your* children, that's what I been too busy doing. Y'know, when Ma was losing it and couldn't hardly recognize a tree from a trailer and nobody'd seen head or tail of that bastard Efstratiou, who was it that dropped their life to come help you, Eleni. Don't interrupt me. You just sit there and be quiet. Sit there and listen to me for once. Now, I don't want nothing for it. I never did. I came back cause this is my family and I'd do it again if I have to. But if you think you're the only one still burnt up about this thing then you just got to think again. You got to find something to do, Eleni. I don't want to be here any more than you do. Honest to God I don't. Far as I'm concerned it'd be better if this old house just burnt its own self to the ground, take all Ma's old shit with it. That basement's overflowing cause you'll never let go of a single speck of dust what might've made Ma's sneeze. I go to work and I come back and during that time my own life happens outside of this house, Eleni. And who asks me about it. Who asks me about my life. My life stops as soon as I get off that bus, and then I'm back to this. So you can make all the cakes you want, Eleni, and hell if I care what you do to that basement. But I am not about to keep leaving myself at this door. And I suggest you clean this up. House oughta be clean for Easter.

Back in the foyer, Evan dropped his brief and overcoat at the door, shut it on its tracks before Kitchen could even come find him. The bed wasn't made. The curtains still drawn. She wants me to clean out the basement, he thought, and she can't even make the bed. Not that it mattered, not really. He sat on the corner of the bed, took a long time unlacing his boots, kicking them aside. He slid a thumb into the cuff of his wool sock, rolled it down slowly. Now he could hear Kitchen's mewling from the other side of the door. He watched her shadow sniffing around under the tracks, exhaled, slid a thumb into the other sock, pulled it off in one long motion. He laid himself back on the bed.

Evan traced tiny cracks in the ceiling paint, illuminated by the end-table lamp. His chest heaved up and down in its own irregular rhythm. He was flushed beneath the heavy sweater. He wanted to take it off but mostly he just wanted to lie there and not think about it. But he had to. How could he not think about it. He did feel a little bit guilty for yelling at his sister, it's true. But she's got to get it together one of these days, he thought. She's got to realize it's none of it easy for anybody. She thinks just cause she's the one got left with kids she's the only one allowed to feel bad. Thinks it's everyone else's job to dress them in the mornings and walk them to the bus and play with them on the weekends. Which of course I don't mind doing it, it's not that. I love them, I do. Love them like my own. But that's just it, Evan thought, slipping a hand absently underneath his sweater, they aren't my own. Are they. And maybe I won't ever have my own, will I. His fingers twisted the hair around on his belly before instinctually sliding under his waistband. It was a small comfort, resting his hand just below his belt, the warmth of moving through the day seeping up from between his legs, the softness of his own pubic hair collecting his scent, small reminders that yes you do have a body and at least that belongs to you. But what do I do with this body, Evan thought. If Josiah were here—but no, that's not right either. What's it matter if Josiah's here or not. He's just a kid. A sweet kid, full of heart, very good to his mother. All things I ought to love. Things I do love about him. But it's not enough. I can't make a husband out of him. Not in the Greek church anyway. Besides who would come. What comes next. What does that life even look like. So he's gonna work at the grocery forever, both of us coming home to one of our mother's houses, us always telling each other don't worry it's fine. But no, it's not even that, is it. Evan pushed his hand down further, his fingers closing around his flesh, cupping his own warmth in his palm. Josiah he's got a whole life right in front of him, Evan thought. A whole youth just crouching there in the bushes waiting for him to walk by. Me, I been through it. Made my mistakes. Or not mistakes maybe, no. But I was him too. This town, these corners, they found me out. They'll find him too. Maybe he won't end up bent over a pool table after-hours with the owner's son, or crouched out behind a woodshed with an old friend's cock on his tongue both of them wondering when will his wife get home. But he will have some version of that. That grey smudge. All of us brush up against it some time or another. And once you do that's it. It's on your hands, Evan thought, fumbling with the clasp of his pants. He felt himself start to unfurl in his fingers, a sweaty bloom he didn't try to conceal. And who am I anyway, Evan thought, to try to keep him from it. He'll find his own shaded corners and bar bathrooms and truck beds and open fields. He'll pick up his own smudge, trade his hues with a handsome stockboy during an overnight shift at the Foodland, or else catch the eye of some burly trucker older than me at a filling station and maybe he'll go to the showers with him or maybe they'll do it in the truck, who's to say, or maybe he'll change his mind and be made to do it anyway. And the whole time his smudge will just get darker and darker. All of us out here brushing up against it. Looking for it, even. Wishing it would show its face sometimes cause then at least it's an answer, Evan thought, running one hand across his chest under the sweater, beginning to stroke with the other, to the what do I do with my body question. He brought his palm to his face, lathered it with warm throat spit, inhaled the smell of himself on his fingers. No, Evan thought, his fingers parting that little tuft of hair between his legs, I don't need Josiah for this. This I can do just fine on my own. Evan tested himself slowly, first just the tip of one finger, up to the joint, slow like Josiah used to do. But he's not here, Evan thought, biting his lip, sliding in up to the knuckle. This

I can take. Me, my own body in my body. Other men's bodies in my body. But nothing comes out of it. Nothing comes out of my body. Nothing I could call my own. My sister she has two whole brand new versions of her own self right there and waiting for her to love them again if only she'd look. And me, Evan thought, inserting another finger, testing himself with a third, his arm moving more rapidly now, his chest heaving, me I'll keep buying them toys and taking them out and calling them mine but they won't be mine just how Josiah he won't be mine but me I can be mine me I'm the only thing can be mine and my own me and my grey smudge my blue mountains my green house my black cat me and my body and my body and my body I get to be a man in this body I get to take men into this body but it's all just a part I'm playing that's all just make-believe all the markers are there the stage is set these walls this house these walls are only so thin and I can only keep calling Kitchen my own for so long and I can only keep calling those kids my own for so long my body it can only do what it does for so long and then that grey smudge it'll have me and we'll never get rid of each other the way people like us do.

When he came, it was much more than he expected. All over his wool sweater, there would be no scrubbing that out. Some of it even got in his hair. He lay there panting, consciously unclenching his toes. His wrist was sore, his fingers stiff. It took him a while to pull them back out. He turned his head towards the nightstand. In the shadows of the room the little lamp glinted off the plastic picture frames hung along the wall. Old family members, women from the islands he'd never know, watching him. It didn't make sense to him either, but he felt he could hear the nails holding tight to the wall.

Upstairs he could vaguely hear the twins moving back and forth across the wood. He knew from the falling light outside that soon it would be time for church. Soon he would have to shower and shave, pull out those nice grey slacks and a fresh button-down. He would have to tame his curls behind his ears as best he could and make sure that his tie was straight. Soon he would get into costume, into character. He would dress the twins and help Thea down the stairs and drive them all the way out to Bristol for the service. He would sing along to the hymns and stand in the back of the church by the narthex and act very happy to see everyone after such a long time away. Yes, he would say, we missed you too, and We're hanging in there, God willing, and No, no lucky lady yet, but you know there's still time for that, and No, I haven't met Mathoula's niece, what's her name again, I'm sure she's a very nice girl.

# CHORUS

Come. Into the walls, where it's safe. You're with us now, and we've no intention to keep you longer than needs be. But right now it's a strange energy in this house. Right now it's something not right. You're better off in here, with us.

The night comes on and the family comes slow. All these years in this house. All the families we seen. Only now it seems too much. We'd look away if we could, but what else is it to see. You can see it yourself. The family dressed for church. The mother on her elbows over the sink. And they leave her just like that, the rest of them, they do. It's a new boy come now at the door we never seen before, in a red pick-up, to collect em all. And there they go, out the house, away. Off to the service without her. And suddenly we're lessened. Not to say a house needs people for it to breathe. A house already it's something made, something built up out the living earth by other living bodies. Houses they allow us to build em. They harbor us gladly and willingly. But these rooms, they never forget. Anything in an old house like this, if yer looking hard enough, it'll tell you what it knows. What it has seen. What it misses, even still.

The house it keeps quiet until.

Sometime in the night, the mother goes making her rounds. We catch her from the windows, the reflections in the glass. See how she stands a long time at the children's door. Even longer at the icons on the wall. She kisses the wood and it flows into us—deep blue dreams of a house drifting downstream between the mountains' shoulders. Dogs barking and barking but where from. She flings herself on to her own mother's bed and who can blame us for crowding. For trying to keep company. But step back, stay with us, we told you it wasn't safe. Eleni she's not alone. Somewhere in the house, we feel her—the other one. She's reaching out, she's trying. We know it. Hell, we all tried ourselves, in our time. And who are we to deny her. Course she can't reach her, not like this. And it's that old grief again, shaking the walls. But where are we to go, what are we to do. The strings, the waters. The light come to break against us.

Come, there's only one place left that's safe. Only one place we might be able to weather this reconnection together. Up, up into the turret at the height of the house. The mother, the daughter, they're coming closer than ever before. The one in the walls—she just might be able to do it. If ever any one among us could, why shouldn't it be her. But still the walls they rattle and O how they shake. This grief between the two. It's bigger'n we ever could of guessed. It stretches its hand all the way out the house. All the way to that vacant lot across the way. Surely you must feel it too. Come, become the windows with us, rattling. Come watch as surely she must be watching from the bedroom downstairs too. Big clouds on their march to steal away the moon. And in the white fire of the moon that fresh ruin starts to lose its footing. Starts releasing its shape. See how it comes apart slow, the roof buckling first. Shoulders holding up too long the burdens of the sky. Next the walls, year by year in a raging grey dust. No, stay, you ought to witness it til the end. Never in all our lifetimes could we of imagined. Plaster and bathwater, wires and brick. The pipes snapping finally like veins. Why, the metal makes a chorus all its own, a drone on the wind for miles. All that time crumbling down, the past gone back to the pool. Down comes the earth to the earth. And O this thundering sadness. The deep purple grieving. The barking dogs. And somewhere at the heart of the house, a light—pulling the house back down. The dust it's still not settled come the sirens.

And all the while, the light. Eleni—your *name* child. The light, the light.

# NOSTOS

It is morning, and Evi Warren is standing in the kitchen, cleaning pears.

A little radio crackles from the countertop—*This is Mark and Kim in the morning at your number one hit music station. Don't go anywhere, we're gearing up for your favorite program, the Sunday Morning Time-Warp! Playing all your favorite hits from the '80s, '90s, and now!*

Evi finishes cleaning the pears, scrapes their thin skins into the sink with a knife. She is half bobbing to the music on the radio, though she doesn't know the song. She wipes her fingers on her pink apron, dressed already in a powderblue Sunday dress. She brushes her curls away with the back of her hand. It has been a while since she last colored her hair, and the light coming in through the kitchen window makes a pale lavender out of her roots. After cleaning the pears she slices them evenly, arranging them on the plate just so. In the pan is the slow crackle of butter on the stove. She forks two slices of square-cut ham into the pan, presses them down as they pop. The kitchen window is open just enough to let the cool October breeze into the house. Even in her house slippers, her toes are chilly. But she likes this feeling. Outside, at the little duplex on the corner across the intersection, her neighbor's son is walking to the street to collect her mail. He waves at her, as he always does if he finds her in the window, and she waves back. They take this to mean, *Tell Yvonne hello, I'll come over for coffee later.* They take *later* to mean, *after you kids have gone back to your new homes.*

*

Upstairs, in the hexagonal room at the top of the turret, Effie and Jr. are making a fort. They have used the two wooden chairs as props to drape their sheets across. Underneath the canopy, they spread their comforters on the floor, using the knit white and blue wool blanket Evi made them to cover up. The light comes through the turret windows on all sides, making a kind of starscape out of their bedsheets. They are gathered around a pile of storybooks from their mother's old bookshelf downstairs, illustrated with big bright colors. Effie has her favorite book about the little girl with the cuckoo clock that never needs winding—the first picture is a city of silver steel and snow and blue lights, all the buildings empty except for one shop with a warm fire in its window. That's where the nice old man in the story lives, the one who makes all those trinkets for the little girl's birthday. Jr. is flipping fast through the pages of *Gods, Monsters, Heroes & Men*, making mental lists of which monsters look the scariest, which heroes look most beautiful. So far Perseus is his favorite—not beefy and bearded like Hercules wrestling the lion, but softer, naked except for the strap of his quiver, wild curls twisting out from under his winged helmet. That a boy like that could kill a monster and still look so calm—.

The quiet is interrupted when they hear footsteps coming up the stairs.

*

*Omorfou'm*, Evi calls up into the house, one hand on the railing, another holding a plate of sliced pears and butterfried ham. *Thes na fas tora?* She climbs the stairs, makes her way down the long hallway, past the icona on the wall, to the children's room at the end. *Baby'm, you hungry?* She stops in the doorway, smiles at the empty room, the stripped beds, the books and toys all strewn about the floor. She looks up at the ceiling as if they both have just shared a secret. *I'm gonna find you,* she says into the hallway. Across the hall, Sophia is still asleep in her own little bed, the door cracked open on its hinges too. Evi pulls it quietly to, then makes her way back down the hallway to her own bedroom. The light coming through the curtains making the whole room blue—robin's egg wallpaper, the sunwashed bedspread, the pale blue radiator creaking like the wind. The door to the turret is wide open. A little rumbling at the top of the house. *I wonder where my babies at,* Evi says as she mounts the stairs. *I'm gonna find you,* she says. The attic giggles back.

*

Sophia Kefalas wakes up to the sound of laughter above her head, the smell of burnt butter. She reaches for her glasses on the bureau, finds the cross still draped around her neck. *Thank you, God*, she whispers, *for another day*. It takes her some time to sit up, to draw the blinds, to let a little light in. The dust almost seems startled awake in the sun. It is Sunday morning, says the calendar—October 28th, Evi's nameday. Sophia sweeps the blankets aside, shuffles to the mirror, where she prepares her *thimiato*—breaking the charcoal, lighting the incense. First she blesses the bedroom window, the world outside, then she crosses the hall to the children's room. What a mess, she shakes her great head. Laughter falls down through the ceiling, and Sophia can't help but smile too. Next she carries the censor down the hall, to the iconostasion on the wall. She sets it down on the chest-of-drawers before the saints, crosses herself, says her morning prayers. *Thank you*, she is whispering again, *for another day*.

She is finishing her prayers when Evi comes down from the turret. *Hi koukla'm*, Evi says to her sister. They kiss each other's cheeks, hands on each other's shoulders. *You don't have to be feeding them ham*, Sophia says, *not if they going to take communion*. Evi waves her hand, *Den mbirazei, yem. I don't have to do nothing.* They laugh. Evi descends the stairwell to the landing, her hand on the rail. She stops by the cuckoo clock on the wall, takes her time puling the weights back up. *Look-it to poulaki'm*, she says as the bird shoots out of its door, singing the 9a.m. song. *You should get ready*, Evi says. *They coming soon.*

*

In the bathroom, the tiles are soft in the morning light. Sophia lets her grey hair fall from its clasp. Undoes her pink nightgown button by button. Coaxes the warm water out from those old pipes. A car pulls up to the curb outside, displacing the gravel. From the small round window, Sophia watches as Eleni and that man come strolling around the back of the house. She is carrying a covered tray. Something sweet for the table after church.

*

*Kalos'to yem, kalos'to!* Evi says, opening the back door to the screened-in porch. *Come in out the cold!*

Eleni steps inside, puffing the black strands away from her flushed cheeks. *Hold on Ma, the tray's hot now,* she says as Evi clasps her face with both hands, covers her in kisses. *Lemme just set this down a minute, Ma, hold on now! Efstratiou, can you gimme a hand.* The tall man comes into the house behind her, his wavy brown hair falling over his eyes. He takes the pan from Eleni, sets it on the kitchen table. *Yiassou Mama*, he says to Evi, before stepping back outside to light a cigarette. Evi nods once, does not try to convince him to come inside. *Here baby'm, lemme help you with that,* she says, pulling her daughter's arms out of her heavy coatsleeves.

*I hope the twins didn't give you any trouble*, Eleni says.

*What trouble*, Evi says, exaggerating her surprise.

*Well*, Eleni says, kissing her mother's cheek, *thanks anyhow. I know they're a handful.*

*My hands is big enough for all a y'all*, Evi says.

The coffee is already on the stove, percolating. Eleni moves to readjust the knob on the radio. *We got to get you a new one a these, Ma. This thing it's older'n you are.*

*I'm still working just fine*, Evi says, pulling out the coffee cups from the cabinet. *Where it's you brother, he supposed to be here too.*

*He's coming, Ma. Don't worry. We got to do something about this dress too, what are you wearing this old thing for.*

Evi swats her hand away. They laugh. The doorbell rings, and upstairs the twins' footsteps are rolling across the wood.

\*

When Evan shows up at the front door, the twins shoot down the stairs to meet him first. He is dressed in a crisp white buttondown, maroon tie peeking out from his camel overcoat. He has tried to tame his curls behind his ears but already they are bouncing loose from the gel. *There's my munchkins*, Evan hollers, scooping up Effie and Jr. into his arms. They are tiny still, easy enough to carry onehanded. *What'dya bring us Evan, huh, what'dya bring!* they shout. *You little bugs aren't getting nothing if you don't hurry up and get dressed for church.*

In the kitchen, Evi is standing ready with her hands out to clutch her son's face. *Hi Ma*, he says, kissing her cheek, *xronia polla, Happy Nameday.*

*Thank you yem*, Evi says, *lemme look at you. So handsome, my boy, my kamaria, my pride!*

*Thanks Ma, you look good too. But what is going on with your hair, mother, it's purple! You got to let me dye it for you again soon.*

*I tried to tell her about that ratty old dress too*, Eleni says. *Tell her, Evan, just look at that old thing! We got to get her some nicer looking dresses for church.*

*Who I'm supposed to look purdy for*, Evi said, her palms outstretched in the air. The twins creep up behind Evan again and she cuts them a secret look. *You hear the way they talking me. I guess you Yiayia she's getting old.*

*Yiayia's not old!* Jr. hollers, and Effie goes *Yeah, she's just Yiayia!*

*You heard that*, Evi says, pouring the coffee. *Yiayia's just Yiayia.*

*Well I know two little bugs gonna get left behind*, Eleni says, *if they don't hurry on up and put some nice clothes on.*

*I don't wanna! I wanna stay with Yiayia*, Jr. says. *Want Yiayia to tell us stories again.*

*Well your Yiayia's coming with you if you'd hurry up and get ready. She can tell you stories at the Bright Star afterward.*

*You know, Ma*, Evan says, *it's tradition you should be taking us out on your nameday, not the other way around.*

*Baby mou, I take you go get whatever you want. Anything it's mine, it's yours. You know that. Sit a while, have some coffee. I take care of the kids.*

\*

Upstairs, Evi is fitting the twins into their Sunday best. *There*, she says, *now you look so sharp.*

*I'm not a shark*, Jr. says, tugging at his collar.

*Yiayia*, Effie says, *will you tell us the story about your nameday again.*

*Yeah*, Jr. says, *the one about the well.*

Evi pulls the twins in close to her hip, running her fingers through their hair. *I tell you as many stories as you want to hear, my babies. You just got to promise Yiayia you gonna remember.*

*We will*, Effie says.

*Yeah*, Jr. says, *and if we forget, you can always just tell it to us again.*

MEMORY ETERNAL

Morning sneaks in quiet, first one finger then another through the crack between the mountains and sky—that thin daymoon disc pecking its way out the blue air. The light drops down and scuttles across the grasses, the concrete. Mist cannot keep it or the water or the pines not even the day can keep itself from starting up again. *Look here, look here* says the day, just as full of what's missing.

The light rolls down the mountains' steep shoulders, across the wide plains and steep valleys until it collides with the boards of the front porch. Morning presses its pink nose close to the glass window, stretches its fingers across the panes, its palms still specked with dew from having brushed the wet air. The light it knocks soft against the metal sconces by the door. It knocks soft against the old wood. And after enough looking the light it lets itself inside.

Now inside the house, the light drags itself into the foyer, still soft and blue, where halfdrawn blinds let a little more through. The dust doing a firefly dance in the sun. All the furniture clinging tight to its plastic coatings. In the center, the cot—blankets bunched in a single mound of fabric. On the nightstand, a folded card. *Happy Mother's Day*. The photos on the wall bristle, unwatched—family members forgotten if not looked at, if not strung up in a row or scattered across beaureaus. Faces of old women, dead women, faces of women when they were still children, balanced on the knees of some other hooded mother long gone down to the dust. A whole cluster of faces in their quiet swarm, the landscapes behind them blending into a reel of unreal earth—the village, the island, a dark room, the island, that very same couch in the foyer. When the light catches their faces from the window the women seem to arch their backs, to flutter away. If they could, they'd lose the wall. The eyes, the women seem to say, where are the eyes. And in the sunbeams, dust comes to settle on their frames, a strange pollination.

The sun is moving higher in the sky, taking the light with it. It has traded its softness for yellow edges, watching the house from up high. It cuts the weathervane to ribbons of metal and shadow, makes trenches of shade between the shingles, the wood. A new entrance this time, through the turret windows. The shutters weighed down with dust. The room empty but slowly filling up with orange light trickling down the staircase through the door left ajar. Washing the big bed, a small disturbance in the sheets. Only half of it made. What bits of gold remain beneath the censor's cake of soot glimmers in the new light. The prayer book open, waiting for those old fingers to find the right hymns. The charcoal in its bag waiting for that Sunday spark. In the white box of the liturgical calendar—May 21, the feast day for Saints Constantine and Helen equal to the Apostles. The pipes groan. No one to quiet them.

Noon is perched now directly above the house. Shadows have flooded back into the upstairs hallway, thick corridor of quiet wood. There is no footpatter against the floorboards. No children tucked behind the coats in the closet or hooking their legs through the banister slats. The cuckoo clock on the wall by the stairs has gone silent. Noon shadows have left it clutching dark space, the pinecone weights low and motionless at the bottom of their chains. All the springwork villagers at rest behind the little wooden doors. There will be no dancing in the square at noon, no chopping of wood at twelve-thirty. The milkmaid, the tinker, the cuckoo bird all waiting for hands to come pull the heavy pinecones back up to the clockhouse.

The sun drags its paper lantern further west, searing an orange gash into the upstairs window where Kitchen's black shape sits pooled on the sill. In her eyes it's the warm concrete glow of the gutted house across the intersection, a metal refuse bin with its fresh blue tarp flapping in the wind. In the light, the iron railing of the side staircase peels off in black flecks. The rusted copper flesh underneath. In the tiny room the light drenches everything—stacks of papers scattered across the desk, tattooed with coffee rings; the futon unfolded; a whorl of sheets hastily uncovered. By the leg of the desk, a small pot is overturned, the little fern scattered across the wood in its own dirt. The light noses down and makes its way inside even this.

Having spent the middle of the day behind the atmosphere the daymoon polishes itself new, a grey pearl in the afternoon blue. The sun it's on a slow track back down to the mouth of the mountains. Curious, the light bends down on its knees, pulling aside the curtains in the children's bedroom. The beds, it sees, are empty. Covers unsoiled but thrown to the carpet floor. All the books still on the shelf, save for one. Facedown on the carpet, a storybook flexes its spine. Across the pages some hero is running towards an army, a beast; some God is becoming an animal; Helen making her way on out to Troy. On the bureau between the beds, Jr.'s treasure—that plastic locomotive, smoke half-billowing from its engine. But there isn't a hand to move it across the carpet, those treacherous arctic plains. No hand to hide it safe inside the tree. The walls, so spoiled on the secrets of children, strain against the quiet. You could almost hear the flowers on the wallpaper growing.

Determined now, the light has made it back into the hallway. At the end of the hall, the iconostasion draped in bronze and dust. The candles all but spent, frayed wicks burnt down to puddles of wax in opaque votives. Cotton swabs of holy oil and smears of ash. Droppers of holy water, lanternshade. The big censor and its quiet bells hung on a tack, cracked open egglike, its incense a crumble of white. Scattered across the top of the black chest-of-drawers, the palms from last year's Sunday. Brittle now, they wouldn't remember desire. The light, now deepening, nails the icons to the wall. A gathering of saints waiting for the lips to murmur their prayers, for the lips to kiss their hands, their feet. At the center, the virgin mother clutching her child, entirely embossed in silver; only their faces are painted on wood, peering out from under their hoods. St. Helen hangs alone, near a separate effigy of herself and her son. In her arms is the true cross, glowing. Where are the hands to relight us, say the candles. Where are the lips to pray.

Against the falling light, the submarine window in the upstairs bathroom still retains its blue. The tiles, little squares of birdshell in the off-white caulk. Leaky faucetheads drip into the babyblue sink, silver pipes, the drain speckled in white. The wooden footstool Effie used to watch the giant squids go by, now upturned on the tile. The window's lattice making spiderweb shadows on a white shower curtain. The pink shower mat still damp.

Out back the big willow drinks her own share of the light, bristling with her first new leaves. Squirrels race between her branches. Somewhere in her hair an unwatched bird crying out. The fence dipping closer and closer to its trunk as the years pile on. Not so long ago the twins spent entire afternoons hiding underneath her branches. Now there are no footprints in the mulch. No plastic in the boughs. A wind comes by and brings a sweep of clouds behind it. Their own atmospheric architecture, a nest of blooming cloud swimming in the blue. Where are the children, asks the roots. Unclear, answers the cirrus. The mesh netting enclosing the screened-in porch behind the house frays blue and purple in the falling light. Nobody has dusted that table in months. Nobody has painted those boards. The trapdoor made for the cat to creep through lets in only small rushes of wind. A rabbit in the bushes tests the air, briefly releases the shade before remembering its size. It ducks quietly back down into its warren.

The light, now caught between an evening purple and orange, sneaks back in from the kitchen window, testing the sturdiness of faucets, countertops. In the kitchen, tiles are boxes of warm cream except for the puddle of shadow where Kitchen now huddles tight against herself, the long swish of her tail sweeping. Unfed, she licks the light from her paws. It drenches the chipped baseboards and the rubber scuffs of the kitchen table's feet. The Frigidaire unit hums and only the pipes answer. In the sink, there is a winestained coffee mug upturned on the drain. A green light beeps every third second from the answering machine. New message, new message. Another call has just come through. The words echo through the empty kitchen—*Just calling to see how she's doing. Call me back when you hear something.*

The light, now peeling back across the sky in a pink ooze, finally unfolds its fingers from around the olive house. It drags itself out the backdoor, across the splintered porch. But as it shambles slowly back away a small piece of the light turns back, one last glance. That sliver of light slips down into the crawlspace between the steps and the earth. That little white storage door. A brief chink in the dirtclotted window. For a moment, the shadows in the basement are illuminated. The gristle of earth and moisture. Cold stone, wooden stairs. The washing machine at the landing, and the echo *Throw it down*. Boxes of wilted vinyl and stacked afghans. Scuttle of small mammals. Television antennae and *Hit it again see if it works*. A Christmas tree leaning out of its box, marked up orange and tiger-red when *Get those markers off the carpet* and *Don't let it topple now* rang. Shelving settled deep into armfuls of boxes, books, bottles of *That was a good year* gone sour. The manual for a jungle-gym never completed propping up the victrola's short leg. Green eagle clutching a clock in its talons, fully stopped. Blankets and blankets. Candles and matchbooks from the thunderstorms, the power outages, *It's just God playing the drums. Big party up in heaven. All that dancing, everyone spilling their drinks*. The vacuum relieved of its dusty bellyful, rags from the *Soak it in vinegar* days. Wall to wall the clutter packed and tossed aside and rearranged to fit the next wave on top of itself even though *You got to go through it Eleni* and *I can't let that go. I can't let that go. Not that. That was Ma's. I can't let that go*. The light blinks out. The old woman steps out of the walls. In the center of the basement, she takes a broom from the clutter and begins to sweep. *I'll get it started for you.*

*Then I'll go.*

*[ Exit ]*

# GRATITUDE PAGES

It's a lot of folks I want to thank here. Folks without whom this object would not exist. Call me sappy if you need to but so be it. I am. Here goes.

## My Mentors

Lea McMahan—For both challenging and nurturing me at the same time, all those years ago, and for your friendship still. For inviting me into my first home outside of home—the stage. For showing me how drama / theater / characters / stories / language / voices are all so intrinsically connected. For trusting me to write, to direct, to make decisions which would impact not just myself but those around me too. For all the wine, and your unmatched love of movies. For making this lonely Tennessee kid feel like there was room somewhere for me too. That there could be a home wherever I went.

Sue Hartman—For giving me my very first copy of *Lord of the Rings*. For seeing the storyteller in me, even at such a young age, and for coaxing that out of me. For being the first person in my life to tell me something I had written was beautiful. For making me believe that. For making me want to become the kind of teacher that you were. My love goes with you everywhere you are.

Jennifer Kates—For teaching me everything I needed to know about fiction, and also for being the first person to say to me *I think you might be a poet*. I didn't know how to take that back then, but now I know you were right. You always did have a knack for sussing us all out. I hope this is just one of many books I'll get to send you in the mail out the blue. You nursed what fragile flame I had back in Middle Tennessee, my most precarious years, and I'm more grateful to you than I can explain. There's a whole world out there, and you made me feel I could step into it.

Michelle Valladares—For taking me seriously as a poet even when I wouldn't. Even when I couldn't. For seeing me. For supporting all my strange and far flung ideas. For believing me about the ghosts. For trusting my gut more than even I knew how to. And for saying, always and with the most limitless warmth, *Yes*. Yes, you do belong here and yes, you have work to do. For teaching me the rules I had to know, and encouraging me (always and on my own terms) to break them.

Cynthia Cruz—For giving me permission to write with where I come from on my teeth. For teaching me that poetry has no business on a pedestal. That nothing is too small or grimy or insignificant for a poem, because a poem is made up of life and life is made up of so much. It's not all beams of sunlight and soaring eagles. Sometimes it's the torn envelope, the heavy sheets of construction mesh, that particular blue flaking off the side of my grandmother's house in Greece. The poems in between each movement of this book were originally drafted in our first workshop together, and they've remained essentially unchanged. I thank you for drawing them out of me, and so much more besides.

David Groff—For being one of the single most warm individuals I have ever known. For those drop-of-the-hat emergency phone calls. For the grumpy coffee and friendly (but serious) advice. For introducing me to Cavafy's work, not realizing (or maybe you did) that his name was also mine. For taking this book just as seriously as any other that could have come across your desk, despite all my insecurities. Yours is a generosity that no tool yet is capable of measuring. I hope to be able to return that, one day.

Václav Paris—For reading more drafts of this book than either of us imagined. For all your sincere engagement, not just with my work but me. For the exclamation marks in your emails, the question marks in my draft margins. For fielding all my ridiculous ideas and for your honesty when I needed to hear it. Quite simply, this book could not have become itself without you. I can't thank you sincerely enough for that. But beyond the book, I thank you for your bright energy, your friendship, for helping me carry the glow around.

To all my other mentors, teachers, and loved ones at City College and beyond. There are so many of you and I'm grateful for you all. If I know you, then this is for you too.

## My Friends

Alex Terrell—Where do I even begin with you, T. First I should thank you for the title of this book. One of our first phone calls after I moved to the city, not a month after my Yiayia had passed. You said *I have this phrase in my head, but I think maybe it's for you*. You were right. Thank you for years of being right. I mean that so sincerely. Thank you for approaching that awkward little kid at orientation all those years ago, so uncomfortably dressed as I was in oversized khakis and boat shoes, the starch in my button-down sticking to my skin in the Tennessee summer. Thank you for asking me to eat with you. For staying up the whole night talking stories and magic and joy. For so many years of stories and magic and joy. For never lying to me about myself. For making me your family. For saying *I need you here* enough that I believed it. I am so proud and so blessed to be in this life with you. *Time, it took us to where the water was*. Just look what the water gave us. I love you with all that I got.

Amanda Dunaway—My Mander, where would I be without you. I guess I have a certain scheming instructor to thank too, for putting us together that first day of class. But I have you to thank for the crazy warm years. For always saying yes to a road trip. For walks to the library and drives through the boro, both of us always taking stock of what used to be where. For all your various couches, whenever I needed them. For all our adventures, yes, but mostly for just sitting in the floor with Clark, doing nothing but together. I can't think of Tennessee without thinking of you. The word home sounds like you when I say it. I love you deep. *Etcerenough.*

For all my other Tennessee folks. The drives on out to nowhere and scary movie marathons. For haunting the local 24hr grocery with me cause there was nothing else to do (until it *became* the thing to do). For the hikes and cigarettes in unfinished cul-de-sacs of the rich neighborhoods at night. I am all of it cause of all of you. This is for you as much as me.

Matt Gahler—Thank you for being beside me, even when I was too shy or embarrassed to ask for help. For tacking up the final movements of this book on the back of the office door, helping me chart the angle of the light. For buying all those books about health when I told you the news (don't think I didn't notice). I love you with my whole haunted heart. *There's a sea of possibilities up there.* Let's go up, up, up.

David Nemat-Nasser—I sometimes forget we haven't known each other forever. Thank you for that cake you made when I finished the first draft—the one with the house carved into the icing. For sharing your own ghosts with me, and believing in mine.

Kat Gelsone—Thank you for reminding me to eat. For being more excited about this book than I was most days. For reminding me grief can be a healthy too, in its way, and for being my encyclopedia for all things Gothic. Love you, crazy dinosaur lady.

Chris Bonfiglio—Thank you for the literal trays of lasagna. For reading those first rough pages and still convincing me to keep going. Also for loaning me all those books you'll never get back (they were more useful than you know).

Joe Nasta—For reading these pages on the other side of the world. For encouraging me to take the leap with this book. And for your own work and friendship. I have such big love for you, there's no word to name it.

For all my City folks—I couldn't think of better company. For all the writing days. For Thanksgiving on Halloween and Halloween on Valentine's. For haunted houses in Portland and holy water in the fridge. For always showing up for each other. Whether you read early pages of this book or not, this is for you too.

## My Family

Blowfish (Victoria Elizabeth Jones)—My sister and my favorite person. Thank you for all the years of hiding under trees, running through the neighborhood, arcade games in the basement, going along with all my wild and stupid little plans when we were kids. Thank you for being someone I can talk to about anything. For giving me better advice than I could ever give myself. For being my best friend my whole life. I don't know how I managed those first four years without you, but I'm glad I can't remember em.

Paul Athanasios Varlan—My brother regardless of biology. For being just as big a goof as I am, and for helping me realize that's a good thing. For all the LOTR marathons and late night ramens. For knowing me better than I know myself, and for always asking me what I'm working on. For always reading it, even if you had to pry it from my anxious hands. Thank you for being the most supportive and constant friend in my life. I love you more than you know.

007 (Peter Coromilas Jones)—For always encouraging me to find my own way. For trusting that I would. For all the bike rides and hikes and adventures. Thank you for always listening to my stories as a kid (God knows I must've made you sit through so many). And thank you for taking them seriously. For listening when I said *This is what I want to do*. For saying, *Go for it, just go for it all the way*. For reading me all those mythology books and fantasy stories as a kid. You gave me the love for stories early, and I couldn't be more grateful for that. Consider this book repayment for that, in it's own way.

Ma (Zena Sfakianos Jones)—This book isn't just *for* you. It's as much a part of you as I am. Thank you for loving me, stubbon as I am. Thank you for the care packages, the warm voicemails. For teaching me how to do Greek folk dances around the living room table as a kid, and forcing me to go to Greek School (I wish I'd of listened to you and stuck it out). Thank you for teaching me to look out for myself. For calling me about your dreams and helping me interpret mine. For praying for the whole family every day, and every other act of selflessness you offer us. You really are my model in so many ways. Thank you for trusting me, even if you didn't always understand what I was up to. For keeping me close to the culture. I love you more than this little paragraph could say, but I hope you'll take it. I hope you'll know I mean it.

Yiayia (Victoria Soliosi Sfakianos)—You told me something once in Greek that I'll never forget. I hope more than anything that this book reaches you somehow. That you know I did it for both of us. You are my entire heart, and I wouldn't be half the person I was without you. I have never felt such a ferocious love. And I hope this book can return it to you, even a little bit. Σ'αγαπώ.

To all my other family across the world—Nouno and Nouna, for being my second parents and showing me more love than I could repay. To all my aunts, uncles, cousins, and family in Tennessee, Alabama, Rhode Island, Mytilene, and anywhere else you may be when you read this—this is also for you, with my love.

Finally, but certainly not leastly, I want to thank my new family at the Operating System. To friends both new and old, and those I haven't yet had the pleasure of meeting. To Robert Balun for your generous but honest eyes, the long phone calls and your general warmth as a person. To Joanna C. Valente, my fellow Greek witchy poet sibling, for your wellspring of love—may my love return to you always. And most especially to Elæ—thank you for your honesty, your absolutely bottomless generousity, and your fierce dedication to the cause. For being a source of disruptive joy in all that you do. I am sincerely grateful.

With love all. Til the next one.

Aman.

# IN STILL ROOMS : A CLOSE-QUARTERS EPIC
## A CONVERSATION WITH CONSTANTINE JONES

*Greetings! Thank you for talking to us about your process today! Can you introduce yourself, in a way that you would choose?*

I'm one of you, whoever you are.

*Why are you a poet/writer/artist?*

I never knew any other way to be. I was it before I knew it was something.

*When did you decide you were a poet/writer/artist (and/or: do you feel comfortable calling yourself a poet/writer/artist, what other titles or affiliations do you prefer/feel are more accurate)?*

I don't know that it was ever a conscious decision. Especially since I used to do so many different things when I was younger. I drew a lot as a kid, I performed in improv theater and short films, I made little comics in my school notebooks etc. I was always telling stories, one way or another. I didn't fully take to writing though until a little later, when I moved to Middle Tennessee for school, and even then all my friends had to tell me I was a poet. Which I find extra funny since this answer is coming at the end of a novel.

Anyway, none of those titles really feel right to me or totally accurate in terms of what I do. I been using the phrase *thingmaker* to describe myself for a number of years now. It makes the most sense to me. I'm at a point in my life / practice now where I'm embracing all urges to combine genres / modes / mediums depending on what the work needs. It also echoes another phrase I been using as a handle for more than a decade now, *stories & noise*, which I think is exactly what I make.

*What's a "poet" (or "writer" or "artist") anyway?*

Most essentially I think a curious person. Someone genuinely inquisitive, dissatisfied with the given answers. The work that resonates with me most,

in any medium, is the stuff that shakes me out of familiarity with things. Work that makes me see the ordinary fresh. Maybe not brand-new, exactly, but differently somehow. It's a really necessary kind of disorientation that I think artists of any medium are charged with offering back to the world.

*What do you see as your cultural and social role (in the literary / artistic / creative community and beyond)?*

The "Western" Anglophone tradition (whatever construct that may be) is ingrained with some very dangerous conceptions about culture. What I mean by that on a personal level, at least, is that anything Greek is largely considered ancient, dead, finished, long-ago. You want to take Greek lessons at a university? You're gonna be translating Homer. Fine, but that's not Modern Greek as it's spoken in the actual country of Greece (let alone all the variations in dialect across regions). Meanwhile you want to take Latin? Fine, you can do that too. But the university might also offer Italian, and you won't have to be in the Classics department to take it. Who are the Greek poets any given reader can think of? Homer, Sappho, maybe one of the playwrights. Ok that was thousands of years ago though, so fast forward. Who are the names now? Both in and out of translation? Both dead and living? And you can do this same type of questioning with Queer writers; with writers from the American South; with writers who share any of my various other particularities.

My whole point in this admittedly circular gripe is just to say—Greek culture is so much more than folks at large give it credit for. There are so many version of *Greek*-ness, of *Southern*-ness, of *Queer*-ness. And it takes someone who comes from all those communities and all those traditions to be able to tell about it right. So if anything, I'd say that's very high on my list of priorities as a contributor to literary culture—of adding one more authentic voice and updated version of these cultures into the mix.

*Talk about the process or instinct to move these poems (or your work in general) as independent entities into a body of work. How and why did this happen? Have you had this intention for a while? What encouraged and/or confounded this (or a book, in general) coming together? Was it a struggle?*

This book started with a phone call from my dear heart Alex Terrell, who gave me the title as a phrase that she thought I might could do something with. I had just moved to New York from Tennessee and my Yiayia (my grandmother I mean my mother's mother I mean my mother two times) had just passed. I was totally unmoored from all my projects, none of it felt worthwhile. So I typed that phrase T. gave me onto a word document and just wrote the first line. I had no idea where it was going or what it was going to become. After a while I started writing poems again more seriously, more deliberately. It was the first time I had worked with Cynthia Cruz and I was sketching out all these neighborhood poems. I couldn't afford a camera back then, hadn't yet saved up for one, so I was taking all these camera phone pictures of my surroundings and trying to do those photos back as poems. After a while they started to congeal, but still it didn't quite work. I was under a lot of internal pressure, I think, to sort of pick a thing to do and do that one thing. It took a while to shake myself out of that, and I'm grateful that I did. Once I made the decision to punctuate the chapters of the novel with these poems, the whole rest of the structure sort of fell into place bit by bit. The addition of the Chorus, the constant interruptions of linear time, the confluence of religion / mythology / superstition etc. All of it made sense once I stopped trying to separate what I was doing into "this" or "that."

*Did you envision this collection as a collection or understand your process as writing or making specifically around a theme while the poems themselves were being written / the work was being made? How or how not?*

The only thing I understood pretty early on in this project was that it was essentially a kind of grief exercise. I'm a project person by nature. Ask any of my friends, they'll tell you. It's very hard for me to write something as a kind of one-off, or standalone. It's always three or four different bodies of work in my head at any given time, which is reassuring to me in the sense that I can just move through my days with all of them at least a little bit on my mind. That way, whenever something comes down to me, I don't worry too much about where it "belongs." I just know that eventually it's gonna get grafted onto one project or another.

*What formal structures or other constrictive practices (if any) do you use in the creation of your work? Have certain teachers or instructive environments, or readings/writings/work of other creative people informed the way you work/ write?*

I am and have always been more inspired by music / sound than anything else, in terms of impulse to create. For me there is always a sonic foundation to the work. For *In Still Rooms*, it was this obsession with the idea of a Chorus—of a collective counterpoint to the Ancient Greek "Hero"; a body both inside and outside the action at once, whose lines were danced, sung, accompanied by drums or the stamping of feet. It's sort of like the first time I read *The Waves* or *Jazz* (and don't get me wrong, I'm no Virginia Woolf and certainly no Toni Morrison), but I *understood* those books. I got them, how they worked, and I felt that they got me too. They're the kind of books that simply could not exist in any other form, as what I can only describe to be works of sound set to language. Hopefully with the slow trickle of my work into the world, what I mean by that will begin to make more sense.

*Speaking of monikers, what does your title represent? How was it generated? Talk about the way you titled the book, and how your process of naming (individual pieces, sections, etc) influences you and/or colors your work specifically.*

I sort of talked about this before, but the title was given to me by a dear friend, as actually so many of my titles have been. Which actually I think is such a sweet, intimate gift. Like, listen, I see you and I know you so well, that here's a phrase I'm entrusting you with, that I think would be safe with you. I liked the ambiguity of *In Still Rooms* as a title—the sort of objectlessness of it all, which is essentially what a ghost story is anyway.

In Greek culture, the concepts of ghosts and memory are particularly intertwined, which is where the segment titles came from. The first act is "Heirloom," which I like for its compoundedness—something handed down that also ties together. Then there's "Mnemosynon," which is both the name of the Greek Orthodox memorial service held for the deceased and also a variation of "Mnemosyne," who in Greek Mythology was named "Memory," and mother to the nine Muses. Look at *The Iliad* or *The Odyssey*, and so many other ancient poems and dramas besides, and they all begin with an invocation to Memory and the Muses, bound as the human storytellers were by having lived only their one life. "Nostos" too is an important Greek word, especially for *The Odyssey*. It implies a return back home, wherever that is. And the final movement, "Memory Eternal," is a translation / echo of the Greek Orthodox hymn for the dead at the beginning of the book. It's actually a really beautiful hymn, sonically, but also in its meaning, which not only calls upon us to remember the departed, but for the Lord to remember them too.

And finally there's maybe the most significant name—Eleni, the Greek name for Helen which means *Light*. Light itself is just as much the "hero" of this book as anyone, maybe even moreso. Light is always moving in / through / around the house, getting caught in the corners, bleaching everything blue. It could be said that the thousand ships launched at Troy were really only pursuing the Light. Light itself is the most ghostly thing— always there, somewhere, even when it's not.

*What does this book DO (as much as what it says or contains)?*

If anything, it grieves with and for anyone who needs it. Takes some of the heaviness off.

*What would be the best possible outcome for this book? What might it do in the world, and how will its presence as an object facilitate your creative role in your community and beyond? What are your hopes for this book, and for your practice?*

I hope this book introduces me to so many other Greek-American thingmakers. I hope it can lodge itself as a missing piece connecting more of us to each other, both within and across generations. I hope it might work to dissolve the barriers between arbitrarily incongruous identites—the Greek, the Queer, the Southern etc. This version of a life exists, and if this book can be testament to that, I'll have done what I came to do.

*Let's talk a little bit about the role of poetics and creative community in social and political activism, so present in our daily lives as we face the often sobering, sometimes dangerous realities of the Capitalocene. How does your process, practice, or work otherwise interface with these conditions?*

This book, and the Greek family certainly, is so essentially communal-centric. When I was first conceptualizing it, a phrase I would come back to often is *a close-quarters epic*. I wanted to make a short, quiet kind of book, without any car chases or rooftop shootouts. I wanted a book where relationship *was* the plot. How do we relate to those around us, family or otherwise? Especially when pushed to psychic / emotional limits. It was plenty of people who told me they thought that more should "happen" in the book. But I maintain that emotions *are* events, and they have consequences not just within our own bodies and minds but externally, in the force with which we touch the world. If anything, I aim to continue telling stories where the main character is We. Is Us. Is Our.

*I'd be curious to hear some of your thoughts on the challenges we face in speaking and publishing across lines of race, age, ability, class, privilege, social/cultural background, gender, sexuality (and other identifiers) within the community as well as creating and maintaining safe spaces, vs. the dangers of remaining and producing in isolated "silos" and/or disciplinary and/or institutional bounds?*

I think so much of this problem has to do with re-framing the language we use to refer to the institution of publishing. It makes no difference whatsoever, for example, for publishers to advertise their eagerness for "inclusivity" because that still implies a power / status imbalance. As in, you xyz other-person-over-there are allowed to come in with "the rest of us." No. That's not the right attitude and it's going to get nothing done. That's why I believe so much in what organizations like OS does, horizontally, not top-down. I can't claim to offer "The Answer" to such a deeply-rooted institutional fault, but I can say that leading by individual example is sometimes the most effective starting point.

*Is there anything else we should have asked, or that you want to share?*

The House is open. Please come in, sit down. Just look at all this room.

## ABOUT THE AUTHOR

Headshot courtesy of Francesco di Benedetto

Constantine Jones is a Greek-American thingmaker raised in Tennessee & currently housed in Brooklyn. They are a member of the Visual AIDS Artist+ Registry & teach creative writing at The City College of New York, where they earned an MFA. They also volunteer in the LGBT Center Archives, where they conduct research on queer Greek-American histories as they intersect with HIV. Their work has been performed or exhibited at various venues across NYC.

# WHY PRINT / DOCUMENT?

*The Operating System uses the language "print document" to differentiate from the book-object as part of our mission to distinguish the act of documentation-in-book-FORM from the act of publishing as a backwards-facing replication of the book's agentive \*role\* as it may have appeared the last several centuries of its history. Ultimately, I approach the book as TECHNOLOGY: one of a variety of printed documents (in this case, bound) that humans have invented and in turn used to archive and disseminate ideas, beliefs, stories, and other evidence of production.*

*Ownership and use of printing presses and access to (or restriction of printed materials) has long been a site of struggle, related in many ways to revolutionary activity and the fight for civil rights and free speech all over the world. While (in many countries) the contemporary quotidian landscape has indeed drastically shifted in its access to platforms for sharing information and in the widespread ability to "publish" digitally, even with extremely limited resources, the importance of publication on physical media has not diminished. In fact, this may be the most critical time in recent history for activist groups, artists, and others to insist upon learning, establishing, and encouraging personal and community documentation practices. Hear me out.*

*With The OS's print endeavors I wanted to open up a conversation about this: the ultimately radical, transgressive act of creating PRINT /DOCUMENTATION in the digital age. It's a question of the archive, and of history: who gets to tell the story, and what evidence of our life, our behaviors, our experiences are we leaving behind? We can know little to nothing about the future into which we're leaving an unprecedentedly digital document trail — but we can be assured that publications, government agencies, museums, schools, and other institutional powers that be will continue to leave BOTH a digital and print version of their production for the official record. Will we?*

*As a (rogue) anthropologist and long time academic, I can easily pull up many accounts about how lives, behaviors, experiences — how THE STORY of a time or place — was pieced together using the deep study of correspondence, notebooks, and other physical documents which are no longer the norm in many lives and practices. As we move our creative behaviors towards digital note taking, and even audio and video, what can we predict about future technology that is in any way assuring that our stories will be accurately told – or told at all? How will we leave these things for the record?*

*In these documents we say:*
WE WERE HERE, WE EXISTED, WE HAVE A DIFFERENT STORY

- Elæ [Lynne DeSilva-Johnson], Founder/Creative Director
THE OPERATING SYSTEM, Brooklyn NY 2018

# a KIN(D)* TEXTS & PROJECTS publication

The Operating System has always understood itself as an explicitly *queer* project: not only insofar as that it was founded, consistently produces work by, and is staffed by primarily queer creative practitioners, but also in its commitment to *queering* the normative forms and expectation of that practice. If to queer something is to "take a look at its foundations and question them," troubling its limits, biases, and boundaries, seeking possibilities for evolution and transformation, then queering is written into the DNA of the Operating System's mission in every action and project, regardless of the orientation or gender of its maker.

However: while all the publications and projects we support encourage radical divergence and innovation, we are equally dedicated to recentering the canon through committing parts of our catalog to amplifying those most in danger of erasure. First, this took to the form of our translation and archival oriented *Glossarium: Unsilenced Texts* series, started in 2016, and in 2018 we made concrete our already active mission to work with creators challenging gender normativity with our *KIN(D)\* Texts & Projects* series. Projects and publications under the *KIN(D)\** moniker are those developed by creators who are transgender, nonbinary, genderqueer, androgynous, third gender, agender, intersex, bigender, hijra, two-spirit, and/or whose gender identity refuses a label.

Titles in this series include:

> HOAX - Joey De Jesus
> RoseSunWater - Angel Dominguez
> In Still Rooms - Constantine Jones
> Sweet and Low: Indefinite Singular - Elæ [Lynne DeSilva-Johnson]
> Intergalactic Travels: poems from a Fugitive Alien - Alan Pelaez Lopez
> A Bony Framework for the Tangible Universe - D. Allen
> Opera on TV - James Lowell Brunton
> Hall of Waters - Berry Grass
> Transitional Object - Adrian Silbernagel
> Sharing Plastic - Blake Nemec
> The Ways of the Monster - Jay Besemer
> Marys of the Sea; #Survivor - Joanna C. Valente
> lo que les dijo el licantropo / what the werewolf told them - Chely Lima
> Greater Grave - Jacq Greyja
> cyclorama - Davy Knittle

# RECENT & FORTHCOMING FULL LENGTH
# OS PRINT::DOCUMENTS and PROJECTS, 2019-20

## 2020

Institution is a Verb: A Panoply Performance Lab Compilation
Poetry Machines: Letters for a Near Future - Margaret Rhee
My Phone Lies to me: Fake News Poetry Workshops as
Radical Digital Media Literacy - Alexandra Juhasz, Ed.
Goodbye Wolf-Nik DeDominic
Spite - Danielle Pafunda
Acid Western - Robert Balun
Cupping - Joseph Han


KIN(D)* TEXTS AND PROJECTS

Hoax - Joey De Jesus
#Survivor - Joanna C. Valente
Intergalactic Travels: Poems from a Fugitive Alien - Alan Pelaez Lopez
RoseSunWater - Angel Dominguez
In Still Rooms - Constantine Jones
Sweet and Low: Indefinite Singular - Elæ [Lynne DeSilva-Johnson]


GLOSSARIUM: UNSILENCED TEXTS AND TRANSLATIONS

Zugunruhe - Kelly Martinez Grandal (tr. Margaret Randall)
En el entre / In the between: Selected Antena Writings -
Antena Aire  (Jen Hofer &  John Pluecker)
Unnatural Bird Migrator - Ariel Resnikoff
Black and Blue Partition ('Mistry) - Monchoachi (tr. Patricia Hartland)
Si la musique doit mourir (If music were to die) -
Tahar Bekri (tr. Amira Rammah)
Farvernes Metafysik: Kosmisk Farvelære (The Metaphysics of Color: A Cosmic Theory of Color) - Ole Jensen Nyrén (tr. Careen Shannon)
Híkurí (Peyote)  - José Vincente Anaya (tr. Joshua Pollock)

# 2019

Ark Hive-Marthe Reed
I Made for You a New Machine and All it Does is Hope - Richard Lucyshyn
Illusory Borders-Heidi Reszies
A Year of Misreading the Wildcats - Orchid Tierney
Of Color: Poets' Ways of Making | An Anthology of Essays on Transformative Poetics
- Amanda Galvan Huynh & Luisa A. Igloria, Editors

## KIN(D)* TEXTS AND PROJECTS

A Bony Framework for the Tangible Universe-D. Allen
Opera on TV-James Brunton
Hall of Waters-Berry Grass
Transitional Object-Adrian Silbernagel

## GLOSSARIUM: UNSILENCED TEXTS AND TRANSLATIONS

Śnienie / Dreaming - Marta Zelwan/Krystyna Sakowicz,
(Poland, trans. Victoria Miluch)
High Tide Of The Eyes - Bijan Elahi (Farsi-English/dual-language)
trans. Rebecca Ruth Gould and Kayvan Tahmasebian
In the Drying Shed of Souls: Poetry from Cuba's Generation Zero
Katherine Hedeen and Víctor Rodríguez Núñez, translators/editors
Street Gloss - Brent Armendinger with translations of Alejandro Méndez, Mercedes
Roffé, Fabián Casas, Diana Bellessi, and Néstor Perlongher (Argentina)
Operation on a Malignant Body - Sergio Loo (Mexico, trans. Will Stockton)
Are There Copper Pipes in Heaven - Katrin Ottarsdóttir
(Faroe Islands, trans. Matthew Landrum)

*for our full catalog please visit:*
https://squareup.com/store/the-operating-system/

*deeply discounted Book of the Month subscriptions
are a great way to support the OS's projects and publications!*
sign up at: http://www.theoperatingsystem.org/subscribe-join/

# DOC U MENT
/däkyəmənt/

First meant "instruction" or "evidence," whether written or not.

*noun* - a piece of written, printed, or electronic matter that provides information or evidence or that serves as an official record
*verb* - record (something) in written, photographic, or other form
*synonyms* - paper - deed - record - writing - act - instrument

[*Middle English, precept, from Old French, from Latin documentum, example, proof, from docre, to teach; see dek- in Indo-European roots.*]

### Who is responsible for the manufacture of value?

Based on what supercilious ontology have we landed in a space where we vie against other creative people in vain pursuit of the fleeting credibilities of the scarcity economy, rather than freely collaborating and sharing openly with each other in ecstatic celebration of MAKING?

While we understand and acknowledge the economic pressures and fear-mongering that threatens to dominate and crush the creative impulse, we also believe that
**now more than ever we have the tools to relinquish agency via cooperative means,**
fueled by the fires of the Open Source Movement.

Looking out across the invisible vistas of that rhizomatic parallel country
we can begin to see our community beyond constraints, in the place where intention meets resilient, proactive, collaborative organization.

Here is a document born of that belief, sown purely of imagination and will.
When we document we assert. We print to make real, to reify our being there.
When we do so with mindful intention to address our process, to open our work
to others, to create beauty in words in space, to respect and acknowledge the strength
of the page we now hold physical, a thing in our hand, we remind ourselves that,
like Dorothy: *we had the power all along, my dears.*

### THE PRINT! DOCUMENT SERIES
*is a project of*
the trouble with bartleby
*in collaboration with*
the operating system

www.ingramcontent.com/pod-product-compliance
Lightning Source LLC
Chambersburg PA
CBHW030331100526
44592CB00010B/655